COWBOY LIFE

COWBOY LIFE
Reconstructing An American Myth

Edited and with an Introduction by
William W. Savage, Jr.

University of Oklahoma Press: Norman

By William W. Savage, Jr.
The Cherokee Strip Live Stock Association (Columbia, Missouri, 1973)

Library of Congress Cataloging in Publication Data
Savage, William W.   comp.
  Cowboy life.
  Includes bibliographical references.
  1. Cowboys—The West—Addresses, essays, lectures.
I. Title.
F596.S24   917.8'03'2   74–5960
ISBN 0–8061–1218–2

To the memory of William Levi Taylor

Preface

This book presents a composite view of the life of the cowboy on the Southern Great Plains—more particularly Texas, Indian Territory, and Kansas—from the 1860's to around 1900. It has reference to the persistence of the cowboy image in American culture, argues in behalf of the mythic qualities of that image, and suggests that, if myths are to be useful, their bases in reality must be understood.

The narratives and photographs herein were drawn from materials in the Western History Collections of the University of Oklahoma Library. Staff members Jack D. Haley, Alice Timmons, Jan Gattis, and Marion Jackson deserve special thanks for their interest and kind assistance.

Thanks are due also to a close friend, Donald C. Master, of Norman, Oklahoma, a careful student of the cowboy in his several manifestations. I have always found Don's conversation stimulating and his ideas worthwhile, and so it will come as no surprise to him to find many of his notions herein.

To Sue and Shane, I am, as ever, grateful.

WILLIAM W. SAVAGE, JR.

Norman, Oklahoma
January 15, 1974

Contents

Illustrations

COWBOY LIFE

Editor's Introduction[*]

The cowboy is the predominant figure in American mythology. More than the explorer, trapper, soldier, or homesteader, the cowboy represents America's westering experience to the popular mind, and his image is everywhere. Accounts of his activities, fictional and historical, comprise substantial portions of publishers' lists. His virtues—and lately his vices—have become standard fare in motion-picture theaters and on television. The National Cowboy Hall of Fame commemorates his exploits, and his mystique is evoked by advertising, popular music, and amateur and professional sports. His latter-day cousin, the rodeo performer, though popular in his own right, has acquired a certain mythic quality through association with what is generally taken to be the historical cowboy.[1]

Yet the cowboy image is not presented cheaply. Little that is done in the cowboy's behalf today would correspond to the pulp sensationalism of the late nineteenth century. In fact, the dimensions of the cowboy myth are suggested by the surprisingly high quality, as well as the number, of books, films, sculpture, and graphic art, devoted to cowboy subjects.[2] If these contributions were somehow to cease this very minute, the cowboy in his various manifestations would nevertheless remain a cornerstone of American culture. Certainly this is an assertion that demands substantiation, but proof of its validity is within easy reach, and from several quarters.

The cowboy's place in American literature is secured, for better or worse, not only by Andy Adams' classic, *The Log of a Cowboy* (1903), but also by more recent novels, which include Frederick

[*] Notes for the Introduction begin on page 14.

3

Manfred's *Riders of Judgment* (1957), Jack Schaeffer's *Monte Walsh* (1963), Benjamin Capps's *The Trail to Ogallala* (1964), Robert Flynn's *North to Yesterday* (1967), J. P. S. Brown's *Jim Kane* (1970), William Decker's *To Be a Man* (1967), and Edward Abbey's *The Brave Cowboy* (1956). As works of serious fiction, these books are receiving increasing critical attention, and perspectives on the cowboy myth are broadened accordingly. Richard W. Etulain has distinguished between western novelists and writers of westerns, and it must be noted that the members of the latter group, which includes Zane Grey, Max Brand, Ernest Haycox, Luke Short, and Frank Gruber, have also received their share of scholarly scrutiny.[3]

Owen Wister produced a book of enduring popularity in *The Virginian* (1902), although, as J. Frank Dobie has noted, his hero was "a cowboy without cows."[4] The Virginian, a strong, silent type, fast with a gun and noted for his line, "When you call me that, *smile!*" contributed much to the popular image of the cowboy (Russel Nye says that Wister invented the cowboy), but as a literary figure he is less representative of either the historical or the stereotypical cowboy than are the characters Rolly Little, Deuce Ackerman, and Les Holden in Zane Grey's *The Trail Driver* (1936).[5] Yet, whatever the critical evaluations of them may be, both books have long publishing histories and have served to keep the cowboy before the public.

Although the cowboy made his appearance early in motion pictures and still rides across the silver screen with some regularity, television has been the most influential medium for the elaboration of the cowboy myth. Local stations hardly discriminate between such rangeland film classics as Howard Hawks's *Red River* (1948) and a host of low-budget celluloid horse operas whose stars have gone on to retirement, character acting, or oblivion. These hoofbeats in the wasteland have been joined by others from weekly television series, and here again the cowboy has been given his due. He has ridden through Matt Dillon's Dodge City in many roles since *Gunsmoke* first appeared in 1955; he was portrayed sympathetically in the popular *Rawhide* series, which ran from 1960 to 1965; and he has been featured in a dozen lesser shows, from the long-running *Bonanza* and its imitators, *Big Valley* and *High Chapparal*, to

4

Warner Brothers' formula westerns *Cheyenne, Bronco,* and *Sugarfoot* and to two 1962 series, *The Wide Country* and *Stoney Burke,* both devoted to fictionalized trials and tribulations of modern rodeo cowboys.

One could hardly sustain the argument that any of these series, except perhaps *Gunsmoke* and *Rawhide* (and even then only occasionally), ever placed aesthetics before action on their lists of primary considerations. But television nevertheless presented an intrinsic image of the cowboy, notably in the old Marlboro cigarette commercials, the spirit of which lives on in a spectacular series of newspaper and magazine advertisements, and in occasional documentary programs and specials. One such special was the Columbia Broadcasting System's 1972 program *Will Rogers' U.S.A.,* which presented James Whitmore in a brilliant characterization, replete with rope tricks, of Oklahoma's famed cowboy humorist. For the occasion Falstaff Beer produced some commercials plugging its brand of liquid refreshment by showing modern cowboys working a little and playing a lot. The commercials drew nearly as much critical comment as Whitmore's performance, but the point is that each left a distinct image of the cowboy in the popular mind, and the effort did not go unnoticed.[6]

It would thus be difficult to imagine the contours of American culture, popular or otherwise, without the figure of the cowboy. It would be equally difficult to imagine a replacement for him. Apemen, spacemen, G-men, and supermen have all tried, at one time or another, to rival his popularity, and they have all failed. This suggests a surprising state of affairs, especially in view of the fact that, historically, the cowboy was an individual of little or no significance.

The cowboy, it must be remembered, was a hired hand, employed to tend cattle, whether on range or trail, and his work was strenuous and dirty, his hours were long, and his pay was minimal. Cowboying required no particular skills beyond the initial ability to sit a horse and pay attention. The state of Texas has made much of the superiority of its native sons in performing the mundane job of cowpunching, but a multitude of frail and pampered easterners, Britons, Frenchmen, and others learned to ride and rope in shorter order and with equal proficiency. The work was simply more tiring than heroic, more boring than romantic.

The evidence suggests that cowpunching, as an occupation, attracted an unfortunate breed of men. With few exceptions they had neither the imagination nor the ability to succeed in business—and the beef bonanza of the 1870's and 1880's made cattle raising in the West just that. The cowboy was distinct from the cattleman, as Lewis Atherton has ably shown, and it was the cattleman, not the cowboy, who provided the capital resources and management ability necessary for the expansion of the range-cattle industry.[7] The cattleman's activities constituted an important phase of western economic development, and to this endeavor the cowboy's activities were peripheral. The cowboy was a wage earner, not a capitalist, and only occasionally did he—or could he—rise above that economic level to acquire land or cattle of his own.

If the cowboy's life was a difficult one, and if the work limited his prospects for economic betterment in an era when fortunes were made and lost overnight, it is perhaps well to ask why cowpunching attracted men. The cradle of the range-cattle industry was post–Civil War Texas, and there livestock dominated the economy, despite depressed conditions at local markets. Little else was available to returning Confederate veterans who sought employment, or to the adolescent sons of men killed in the war. With the beginning of the long drives, first to railheads in Missouri and Kansas and later to feeding grounds in Wyoming and Montana, the cowboy life seemed to offer adventure and an opportunity to go somewhere, anywhere. The populations of western communities were more sedentary than their proximities to a geographical frontier might suggest, and those communities were remote from each other. Travel, no simple matter, was expensive. Cowboying offered escape at someone else's expense. It replaced one kind of boredom with another by substituting the trail for the pasture and the plow.

The cattle business and the cowboy life were hardly the stuff of which legends are made, but they did produce America's most potent myth, and it is from this circumstance that the cowboy derives his significance. The cowboy is a symbol for many things—courage, honor, chivalry, individualism—few of which have much foundation in fact. But the cowboy is today less important for what he was than for what he is thought to have been. His symbolism reflects much of America's image of itself. The historian argues in vain

that to know what we are we must know what we were. The eleva-
tion of the cowboy to the realm of myth suggests that, while we may
or may not know what we are, we care less about our documented
past than we do about romantic speculation on the subject of what
our past might have been.[8]

The cowboy, of course, had not the wherewithal to make a hero
of himself. Charlie Siringo, "Teddy Blue" Abbott, and others tried,
and, while they produced interesting memoirs, their works, like their
lives, failed to reach heroic proportions. Cowboy elaborations on the
truth possessed a tinsel glitter that quickly tarnished under intensive
scrutiny. In historical perspective their authors seem to have been
little more than men in a state of arrested adolescence. But such
books are important because they reveal the psychological construct
of the cowboy; that is, they tell us what he thought of himself and
the work he did. Andy Adams managed to record the same information, but without artifice, in *The Log of a Cowboy*, an important
social document that is in many ways a great book. At bottom,
however, *The Log of a Cowboy* brings into focus the disparity between the historical cowboy and the idealized mutation of him that
is so popular, and it explains much about the growth of the cowboy
myth.

Adams sought to tell the truth and succeeded to an admirable
degree. His work was partly autobiographical and assimilated much
that he knew of the experience of others.[9] *The Log of a Cowboy* was
a novel, but it had no plot. It was an accurate portrayal of cowboy
life, centering on a cattle drive from the Río Grande to northwestern
Montana in 1882. Because cowboys were dull, the book also was
dull. As one critic has observed, Andy Adams was simply "too true
to be good."[10] The cowboy has become, in the twentieth century, a
mythical, legendary, and altogether unrealistic character largely
because writers, avoiding Adams' premise that the subject deserved
truth, decided to write interestingly about him. The results have
been various narrative styles that for the most part fall squarely between the stools of elaboration and fabrication and a body of literature in which each contribution builds solidly on the misinformation
supplied by the one that preceded it.

But these were later developments, capping efforts by promoters in the late nineteenth century to make the cowboy a salable

commodity, the first step in the mythmaking process. William F. Cody was among the first to attempt such a thing, and the involvement of the general public in the practice of cowboy worship during the last ninety years attests to his success. Cody took a six-foot, five-inch Texas cowpuncher named William Levi Taylor and in 1884 introduced him to the audiences of Buffalo Bill's Wild West as Buck Taylor, "the King of Cowboys." Buck Taylor thus became the first bona fide cowboy hero.

Cody's action was significant for several reasons. Before his promotion of Buck Taylor as a featured performer in his show, cowboys had experienced what publicists term a bad press. They were, to the journalists of the day, drunken rowdies who, while professing the sanctity of the cow, had no regard for private property or the right of city folk to pursue a life of peace and quiet. They occasionally terrified unsuspecting travelers and tormented greenhorns. Often their employers, acting through the stockmen's associations that brought some semblance of organization to the range-cattle industry, were forced to condemn such actions and to attempt curbing cowboy rambunctiousness.[11] Cody's careful management of Taylor's career as an entertainer did much to alter the public's perception of cowboys. He portrayed the young Texan as a wistful soul who seemed to be longing to return to the bucolic environs of the Great Plains. Promotional literature assured the public that Taylor, despite his size, was a gentle fellow who liked children.[12]

Under this kind of guidance Taylor's popularity increased, and so did interest in the cowboy. In 1887 both received additional exposure through the publication of Prentiss Ingraham's *Buck Taylor, King of the Cowboys; or, The Raiders and the Rangers: A Story of the Wild and Thrilling Life of William L. Taylor* in Beadle's Half-Dime Library. Taylor, the first cowboy hero in fact, thus became, according to historian Don Russell, the first cowboy hero in fiction.[13] Four years later Taylor's name was still a salable item, and the prolific Ingraham was producing thrillers that saw the Texan captured by Comanches (to be rescued by the redoubtable Buckskin Sam) and leading his own group of jovial and honorable cowboys. The character of the cowboy was appearing more and more frequently in popular fiction.

What Cody, Taylor, and Ingraham began was consolidated by Owen Wister, Emerson Hough, and others after the turn of the century. Whether they were showmen or writers, these promoters shared one common characteristic: they presented the cowboy in a context altogether divorced from historical reality. If Wister was not solely responsible for inventing the cowboy, he did establish at least one important literary convention by introducing into the western story a fair damsel for his hero to love. To Andy Adams the cattle trail was a no woman's land, but Emerson Hough sent Taisie Lockhart with a herd and some dutiful cowboys to Abilene in *North of 36* (1923).[14] Ladies of this stripe were, of course, chaste and pure, thin-skinned, durable to a point, but dependent upon the brains and brawn of the male to save the day. Beyond whatever function they served as romantic interests for cowboy heroes—their presence always foreshadowed the typical as-the-sun-sinks-in-the-West happy ending—the ladies allowed trail bosses and cowhands alike to demonstrate just what gentlemen they really were. Rough language disappeared in the presence of a comely belle, and even the most trail-hardened hombre would blush at the slightest attention from a member of the fair sex. As writers of genre fiction, Wister and Hough were not alone in their traditional Victorian portrayal of women. The interesting thing is not that they placed women on pedestals but that they propped up the cowboy beside them.

The emergence of the cowboy, together with renewed popular interest in historical fiction (and continued interest in melodrama), advocacy of the strenuous life typified by Theodore Roosevelt, and the influence of Progressive Era thinking, accounted for the growth, development, and spread of the "western" as a literary form in the early years of the twentieth century.[15] As the heyday of the cowboy, roughly the period between 1865 and 1890, receded in time, the myth of the cowboy grew. Sophistication in writing and the changing tastes of the reading public prompted alterations and modifications in literary conventions. Those saccharine ladies of the range either fell beside the trail or were replaced by crustier members of the sisterhood—erstwhile cowgirls with moxie. More dramatic, however, was the cowboy's literary transformation from hired hand to gunhand. This happened quickly, as soon as writers realized how dull the cowboy was as subject matter for works of fiction. The configurations of western plots for the last seventy-five years demonstrate the success of that transformation.

By taking up the gun, the cowboy ensured his future as America's most persistent, and therefore most significant, myth. The cowboy in fiction thenceforth carried his action on his hip, so that even the most pedestrian western plot could be enlivened by a little zesty gunplay. The cowboy hero used his weapon on the side of good, thwarting evil with a hail of righteous lead that punctuated his drawled homilies. Shooting more and talking less was a rule of thumb in cowboy books and films until the 1950's, when the "psychological western" turned things the other way around, producing cowboys that talked more than ever before. In addition, the psychological slant allowed the good guy to plug the bad guy in the back from time to time without risking his status as hero. This rangeland *realpolitik* made for interesting reading and was enhanced in motion pictures by advances in the chemistry of synthetic blood and developments in film technique.[16] (Eventually, however, the new technology negated the impact of the psychological western movie. Gunplay is louder and more decisive than talk, and in Technicolor it is ever so much more picturesque. Interpersonal relationships now regularly conclude with actors oozing red in the sawdust or the sod.)

Nowadays the cowboy and the gunfighter are virtually inseparable in the western, be it novel or film. Characters, regardless of their occupation, dress like cowboys and wear sidearms. They ride horses and carry ropes. They demonstrate similar traits of character and personality. The cowboy, historically once unpopular and seemingly unsavory, has thus become supremely interesting. The eye is drawn to him because he packs iron, and one never knows when he will cut loose and shoot something or somebody. He is still largely fun-loving and at least partly honorable, but he is considerably more dangerous than he used to be. He stands ready to demonstrate the ability that Americans throughout their history have longed to possess—the ability, in time of crisis, to reach the ultimate resolution.[17]

Violence has a certain fascination for American readers and moviegoers, spectators at automobile races and football games, and viewers of television news. Engineering and the technology of visual media have not created this distinctive American mentality; they have merely exploited it for private gain. Agents of this exploitation acquired the cowboy early and made him over into something useful as entertainment. He is nevertheless important to us because of his place in our conceptions of our past. We would prefer that he be interesting, not dull; decisive, not irresolute; guiding events, not being led by them; free, not bound; self-sufficient, not dependent. In short, we want him to be as little like us as possible. And, considering the cowboy's mythic stature and his integration into American culture, the producers of westerns, whatever the medium, have by and large given us what we want.[18]

This may appear to suggest a sorry state of affairs, especially within the context of the national experience of a people who pride themselves on their heritage and their penchant for truth and who underscore that pride with the most remarkable record-keeping machinery the world has ever seen. It suggests that we have allowed ourselves to be deluded about an important part of that heritage. To some extent, these things are true. But America must have its myths. The nation has a relatively brief history, with little time to develop a culture that has much genuine substance. Thus glorification of the cowboy is necessary. And everything that has been done to the cowboy has been done, consciously or unconsciously, to make him usable as a myth.

That the mythmaking process has been abused occasionally by overzealous writers is hardly evidence that the process itself is not worthwhile. The problem is that, except in a few notable cases, the cowboy has been used to poor advantage. As myth or legend the cowboy could be considerably better than he is.

The cowboy already has public acceptance. Indeed, he is an American fixture. Writers who deal with him need no longer struggle to make him respectable, and it is to be hoped that the best among them will begin to elaborate upon his image rather than simply recreate stock plots and standard characterizations. The cowboy witnessed many events of epic proportions, events significant in the westering experience, but surprisingly few writers have capitalized on this fact in presenting the fictional cowboy in any valid context of historical time.

A case in point concerns the long drive in western fiction—and here it is necessary to consider both western writers and writers of westerns because of their common theme. A survey of seven novels, selected at random, all having to do with trail driving, reveals some interesting facts. The books, Adams' *The Log of a Cowboy*, Hough's *North of 36*, Grey's *The Trail Driver*, Capps's *The Trail to Ogallala*, Flynn's *North to Yesterday*, Mel Marshall's *Longhorns North* (1969), and William Dale Jennings' *The Cowboys* (1971), may be summarized in this manner:

1. All but *North to Yesterday* present action that is precisely defined in time and space; for example, in Grey's book the outfit is moving from San Antonio to Dodge City in 1871.

2. All but *North to Yesterday* reflect attention to history, although not necessarily to detail, and this attention is revealed in historical notes, interpolated philosophical statements, bibliographical notes, and dedications.

3. All but *North to Yesterday* demonstrate a straightforward literary style, wherein the story begins at the beginning and proceeds unswervingly to the end, unembellished by any particular felicitation or sophistication.

In other words, six of seven authors ignored the fictive possibilities afforded by the long-drive motif. This is not to say that they were unaware of them—simply that they ignored them. First, the long drive offers a certain flexibility, of which few authors have availed themselves. It obviates, for example, the need for extensive scene setting. It is no more necessary to explain that cattle are on their way to market than it is to explain that cowboys are taking them there. And it is not necessary to explain, as some have done in great detail, where the cattle came from and precisely where they are going. Unless he is from another planet, the reader understands exactly what is happening. The writer is thus free to create literature.

The immediate orientation afforded the reader by the long-drive motif suggests also that authors could vary the form of their narratives. The historical long drive was an event possessed of many epic qualities. It was a quest for something, and quest stories, comprising a category well known to students of literature, date back at least to Homer. Why, then, could not the novels that deal with it assume aspects of the epic form? Of the long-drive novels considered here, only Flynn's *North to Yesterday* begins *in medias res*, or in the middle of things, as all epics once did. If the subject of the cowboy is worth discussion—and we have established that it is—then it deserves the best and most sophisticated of literary treatments, even by writers who write only to make money. And their purpose should be to produce literature, not reproduce history, for there are already sufficient numbers of historians to do that.[19]

Before this goal can be achieved, however, there must be a return to the sources of the historical cowboy. There must be an attempt to discover the best of that creature, which is to say his qualitative limits, whether those be concerned with his capacity for good or his potential for evil. Myth can, of course, arise from mediocrity, but if it does, it seldom survives for long. We must turn the cowboy inside out and learn more about him. He is already accepted, but now that acceptance must be elevated to some rational plane.

Perceptive men realize that this will be no easy matter. Motion-picture director Sam Peckinpah, who has devoted some time to the analysis of the cowboy psyche, once remarked, "When we can't live something, we try to re-create it."[20] The nineteenth-century cowpuncher's life cannot be lived in the twentieth century, but frequent attempts are made to re-create it, and always for purely selfish reasons. The making of films gives directors and actors vicarious pleasure, even if the results fail to transport viewers to another time. Driving a token number of cattle north along a superhighway to commemorate some long-past event satisfies the egos of organizers and participants. And even the modern cowboy, who sees himself as the latest rider in an unbroken procession of mounted herdsmen, links himself to the historical cowboy to have an individual sense of belonging to something, to some valid tradition.[21] Such endeavors are fruitless, because, while myths can be created and perpetuated, they cannot be participated in, at least not a century after the fact.

It is to these problems that the following selections are addressed. Through the eyes of his contemporaries, the historical cowboy may emerge anew and, it is hoped, to better purpose. Certainly the activities of no other western figure are as well documented as those of the cowboy. The written record is full and varied. The photographic record is substantial and is "as legitimately factual as a canceled check."[22] Altogether, the material is rich and virtually unmined. J. Frank Dobie once wondered whether or not the "literature of the range" would ever mature.[23] These sources suggest that it can, and therefore they warrant careful attention.

NOTES TO INTRODUCTION

1. Joe B. Frantz and Julian Ernest Choate, Jr., *The American Cowboy: The Myth and the Reality* (Norman, University of Oklahoma Press, 1955), 3–14; James E. Serven, "National Cowboy Hall of Fame and Western Heritage Center," *Arizona Highways*, Vol. XLVI (October, 1970), 38–39; J. P. S. Brown, "Cowboy–1970," *Arizona Highways*, Vol. XLVI (October, 1970), 36–37, 42–44; [Gerald C. Lubenow], "Rodeo: The Soul of the Frontier," *Newsweek*, October 2, 1972, p. 27; Bill C. Malone, *Country Music U.S.A.: A Fifty-Year History* (Austin, University of Texas Press, 1968), chap. 5; Jay Cocks, "Overreacher," *Time*, April 17, 1972, p. 91; and Arthur Knight, "The New Old West," *Saturday Review*, July 29, 1972, p. 70. The cowboy is so typically American and so embedded in the national folklore that some scholars, perhaps motivated by the civil-rights movements of the 1960's, have felt constrained to point out that he sometimes came in colors other than white. See Philip Durham and Everett L. Jones, *The Negro Cowboys* (New York, Dodd, Mead & Company, 1965). The mythic qualities of the cowboy are further analyzed and explained in Douglas Branch, *The Cowboy and His Interpreters* (New York, D. Appleton and Company, 1926); Mody C. Boatright, "The American Myth Rides the Range," *Southwest Review*, Vol. XXXVI (Summer, 1951), 157–63; David B. Davis, "Ten Gallon Hero," *American Quarterly*, Vol. VI (Summer, 1954), 111–25; George Bluestone, "The Changing Cowboy: From Dime Novel to Dollar Film," *Western Humanities Review*, Vol. XIV (Summer, 1960), 331–37; and Kenneth J. Munden, "A Contribution to the Psychological Understanding of the Cowboy and His Myth," *American Imago*, Vol. XV (Summer, 1958), 103–47. Instructive on the subject of the rodeo cowboy is Clifford P. Westermeier, *Man, Beast, Dust: The Story of Rodeo* (Denver, World Press, Inc., 1947).

2. See, for example, three outstanding instances of cowboy bookmaking: Bart McDowell, *The American Cowboy in Life and Legend* (Washington, D.C., National Geographic Society, 1972); John Meigs (ed.), *The Cowboy in American Prints* (Chicago, Swallow Press, 1972); and William H. Forbis and the Editors of Time-Life Books, *The Cowboys* (New York, Time-Life Books, 1973). See also Ed Ainsworth, *The Cowboy in Art* (New York, World Publishing Company, 1968); and Ron Butler, "The Big Boom in Western Art," *Arizona Highways*, Vol. XLVIII (March, 1972), 40–44.

3. Richard W. Etulain, "Research Opportunities in Western Literary History," *Western Historical Quarterly*, Vol. IV (July, 1973), 263–72. See also Richard W. Etulain, *Western American Literature: A Bibliography of Interpretive Books and Articles* (Vermillion, S. Dak., Dakota Press, 1972). That scholarly scrutiny of cowboy fiction may be interpreted in more ways than one is apparent in Don D. Walker's two articles, "The Rise and Fall of Barney Tullus," *Western American Literature*, Vol. III (Summer, 1968), 93–102; and "The Love Song of Barney Tullus," *Western Humanities Review*, Vol. XXVI (Summer, 1972), 237–45.

4. J. Frank Dobie, *Guide to Life and Literature of the Southwest* (rev. ed., Dallas, Southern Methodist University Press, 1952), 124. Hereafter cited as *Life and Literature*.

5. Russel Nye, *The Unembarrassed Muse: The Popular Arts in America* (New York, Dial Press, 1970), 289.

6. Robert Lewis Shayon, "Resurrection of a Poet Lariat," *Saturday Review*, April 1, 1972, p. 22.

7. See Lewis Atherton, *The Cattle Kings* (Bloomington, Indiana University Press, 1961).

8. See William H. Hutchinson, "The Cowboy and the Class Struggle (or, Never Put Marx in the Saddle)," *Arizona and the West*, Vol. XIV (Winter, 1972), 321–30; and William W. Savage, Jr., "Western Literature and Its Myths: A Rejoinder," *Montana: The Magazine of Western History*, Vol. XXII (October, 1972), 78–81.

9. Adams' philosophy and method are described fully in Wilson M. Hudson, *Andy Adams: His Life and Writings* (Dallas, Southern Methodist University Press, 1964).

10. Donald C. Master, "Lost Paradise: The Cult of the Cowboy," unpublished paper, p. 10.

11. Gene M. Gressley, *Bankers and Cattlemen* (New York, Alfred A. Knopf, Inc., 1966), 125.

12. Don Russell, *The Lives and Legends of Buffalo Bill* (Norman, University of Oklahoma Press, 1960), 305.

13. *Ibid.*, 305–306; Albert Johannsen, *The House of Beadle and Adams and Its Dime and Nickel Novels: The Story of a Vanished Literature* (Norman, University of Oklahoma Press,1950), I, 277.

14. According to J. Frank Dobie, the success of *North of 36* prompted Hough to advise Adams "to put a woman in a novel about trail driving. . . . Adams replied that a woman with a trail herd would be as useless as a fifth wheel on a wagon and that he would not violate reality by having her." In Dobie's opinion the best character in *North of 36* was Old Alamo, the lead steer. Dobie, *Life and Literature*, 107–108.

15. See Richard W. Etulain, "Origins of the Western," *Journal of Popular Culture*, Vol. V (Spring, 1972), 799–805.

16. The subject of synthetic blood is a fascinating one. It is discussed briefly in Roger Field, "The Technology of TV Violence," *Saturday Review*, June 10, 1972, p. 51.

17. Critics of cowboy productions often do not see eye to eye on the wisdom of ultimate resolutions. See, for examples, Jay Cocks, "Growing Up Absurd," *Time*, January 31, 1972, p. 40; and Arthur Knight, "Boys Will Be Boys," *Saturday Review*, March 18, 1972, p. 20. Both are reviews of Mark Rydell's film *The Cowboys*.

18. Occasionally they do so after telling us that we do not want it. Instructive is Dick Richards' 1972 film *The Culpepper Cattle Co.*, in which a wizened cook tells a young boy, "Cowboyin' is somethin' you do when you can't do nothin' else." Thereupon the film's cowpunchers proceed to have a high old time cursing, lying, drinking, and killing before they die in a blaze of gunfire and glory in a noble and virtuous cause. They are buried in the strains of "Amazing Grace." Cocks, who abhorred the same thing, less picturesquely done, in Rydell's *The Cowboys* a scant three months before, thought it was just fine. See Jay Cocks, "Mixed Company," *Time*, May 8, 1972, p. 94.

19. An interesting recent use of the long-drive motif may be found in Clair Huffaker, *The Cowboy and the Cossack* (New York, Trident Press, 1973), a novel about some American cowpunchers' participation in moving a herd of cattle across Siberia in the 1880's. The *New York Times Book Review*, July 15, 1973, 17, could but wonder aloud what the Russians would think of "this odd hybrid." Zane Grey transported a pair of cowboys to Australia for a similar undertaking in *Wilderness Trek* (New York, Harper & Row, 1944).

20. Interview, KOCO-TV, Oklahoma City, March, 1972.

21. The Historical Performance Society of Waco, Texas, sponsored a drive of forty-three longhorn cattle north from San Antonio to Dodge City, Kansas, in the

summer of 1972. *Sunday Oklahoman* (Oklahoma City), August 20, 1972. McDowell, *The American Cowboy in Life and Legend,* obscures the distinction between the historical cowboy and his latter-day counterparts and has been praised for it by cattlemen who see no difference between themselves and the cowhands of the past. See the comments in *Persimmon Hill,* Vol. III, No. 3 (1973), 84–85; and compare them with the review of Forbis, *The Cowboys,* which appeared in *Persimmon Hill,* Vol. III, No. 4 (1973), 56–57. See also C. L. Sonnichsen, *Cowboys and Cattle Kings: Life on the Range Today* (Norman, University of Oklahoma Press, 1950). The popular desire to identify with cowboys is reflected in any issue of the *Dude Rancher Magazine,* published by the Dude Ranchers' Association, Billings, Montana, and in sales figures for western apparel in *Tack 'n Togs Dealer Roundup Report No. 2* (Minneapolis, Miller Publishing Company, 1972), 3–6.

22. The simile is Margaret Bierschwale's, in *Southwestern Social Science Quarterly,* Vol. XXXVII (June, 1956), 71.

23. Dobie, *Life and Literature,* 92.

Joseph G. McCoy

"Anger and bad whiskey urge him on to deeds of blood and death"

1874

Joseph G. McCoy is remembered in the annals of the western range-cattle industry as the man who opened the cattle market at Abilene, Kansas, in 1867. A businessman, he was critical of cowboys and the way they lived. This selection is taken from his book *Historic Sketches of the Cattle Trade of the West and Southwest,* the first published history of the cattle business.

The herd is brought upon its herd ground and carefully watched during the day, but allowed to scatter out over sufficient territory to feed. At nightfall it is gathered to a spot selected near the tent, and there rounded up and held during the night. One or more cowboys are on duty all the while, being relieved at regular hours by relays fresh aroused from slumber, and mounted on rested ponies, and for a given number of hours they ride slowly and quietly around the herd, which, soon as it is dusk, lies down to rest and ruminate. About midnight every animal will arise, turn about for a few moments, and then lie down again near where it arose, only changing sides so as to rest. But if no one should be watching to prevent straggling, it would be but a short time before the entire herd would be up and following off the leader, or some uneasy one that would rather travel than sleep or rest. All this is easily checked by the cow-boy on duty. But when storm is imminent, every man is

From Joseph G. McCoy, *Historic Sketches of the Cattle Trade of the West and Southwest* (Kansas City, Mo., Ramsey, Millett & Hudson, 1874), 132–42.

required to have his horse saddled ready for an emergency. The ponies desired for use are picketed out, which is done by tying one end of a half inch rope, sixty or seventy feet long, around the neck of the pony and fastening the other end to a pointed iron or wooden stake, twelve or more inches long, which is driven in the firm ground. As all the strain is laterally and none upward, the picket pin will hold the strongest horse. The length of the rope is such as to permit the animal to graze over considerable space, and when he has all the grass eat off within his reach, it is only necessary to move the picket pin to give him fresh and abundant pasture. Such surplus ponies as are not in immediate use, are permitted to run with the cattle or herded to themselves, and when one becomes jaded by hard usage, he is turned loose and a rested one caught with the lasso and put to service. Nearly all cow-boys can throw the lasso well enough to capture a pony or a beef when they desire so to do. Day after day the cattle are held under herd and cared for by the cow-boys, whilst the drover is looking out for a purchaser for his herd, or a part thereof, especially if it be a mixed herd—which is a drove composed of beeves, three, two and one year old steers, heifers and cows. To those desiring any one or more classes of such stock as he may have, the drover seeks to sell, and if successful, has the herd rounded up and cuts out the class sold; and after counting carefully until all parties are satisfied, straightway delivers them to the purchaser. The counting of the cattle, like the separating or cutting out, is invariably done on horseback. Those who do the counting, take positions a score of paces apart, whilst the cow-boys cut off small detachments of cattle and force them between those counting, and when the bunch or cut is counted satisfactorily, the operation is repeated until all are counted. Another method is to start the herd off, and when it is well drawn out, to begin at the head and count back until the last are numbered. As a rule, stock cattle are sold by the herd, and often beeves are sold in the same manner, but in many instances sale is made by the pound, gross weight. The latter manner is much the safest for the inexperienced, for he then pays only for what he gets; but the Texan prefers to sell just as he buys at home, always by the head. However, in late years, it is becoming nearly the universal custom to weigh all beeves sold in Northern markets.

Whilst the herd is being held upon the same grazing grounds,

Buck Taylor July 20th, 1886

William Levi "Buck" Taylor, the first cowboy hero, in a studio portrait
dated July 20, 1886. Under William F. Cody's tutelage the young Texan
was the first to make the cowboy image palatable to the general public.
All the photographs in this book are reproduced through the courtesy of
the Western History Collections, University of Oklahoma Library.

Buck Taylor, shown wearing fancy chaps, embroidered jacket, watch fob, stickpin, and pistol, in a souvenir photograph.

The King of the Cowboys, sporting more practical attire, a Bowie knife, and a wistful expression, reclined on his saddle and a studio stump for this souvenir of Buffalo Bill's Wild West.

Charles A. Siringo, the cowboy author, displaying his revolver. Siringo wrote to make money and dressed accordingly.

Andy Adams, author of *The Log of a Cowboy*, the foremost work of cowboy fiction.

A cowboy at work on a Kansas ranch—a stereoscopic view giving a feeling of depth and an entree into the American home.

Cowboy Trading with Indians — Sign Language.

Copyright 1909 by
Martin Post Card Co

"Cowboy Trading with Indians—Sign Language," announced the caption on this 1909 postcard, which demonstrated that cowboys indeed had to do with Indians. The well-armed cowboy, a pistol in his belt and a rifle across his saddle, sports chaps, suspenders, and a hatband marked "46" and "D/D," perhaps representing the brands of outfits for which he has ridden.

"Chuck Time" on Oklahoma's famed 101 Ranch, where the cowboy endured as a showpiece—a participant in a traveling "Wild West" show, an anachronism for the perusal of tourists. These hands, including the cowgirl mounted at right, are dressed more for show than for utility.

often one or more of the cow-boys, not on duty, will mount their ponies and go to the village nearest camp and spend a few hours; learn all the items of news or gossip concerning other herds and the cow-boys belonging thereto. Besides seeing the sights, he gets such little articles as may be wanted by himself and comrades at camp; of these a supply of tobacco, both chewing and smoking forms one of the principle, and often recurring wants. The cow-boy almost invariably smokes or chews tobacco—generally both; for the time drags dull at camp or herd ground. Their is nothing new or exciting occurring to break the monotony of daily routine events. Sometimes the cow-boys off duty will go to town late in the evening and there join with some party of cow-boys—whose herd is sold and they preparing to start home—in having a jolly time. Often one or more of them will imbibe too much poison whisky and straightway go on the "war path." Then mounting his pony he is ready to shoot anybody or anything; or rather than not shoot at all, would fire up into the air, all the while yelling as only a semicivilized being can. At such times it is not safe to be on the streets, or for that matter within a house, for the drunk cow-boy would as soon shoot into a house as at anything else. Many incidents could be told of their crazy freaks; and freaks more villainous than crazy, but space forbids, save one only. In 1868 a party of young men mostly residents of Abilene, numbering six or seven, were returning from a walk, at a late hour, when all of a sudden they heard the footsteps of a running pony, each moment coming nearer. Before they could scarce divine the meaning thereof, a mounted, crazy, drunk cow-boy was upon them. Yelling in demoniacal voice to halt; adding horrible oaths, abuse and insult. Before the young men fully comprehended the situation, the cow-boy was rushing around them at a furious rate of speed, firing both his revolvers over their heads in the darkness, demanding an immediate contribution from each one of a ten dollar note, swearing instant death to every one who refused to comply at once with his request.

The party of young men were entirely unarmed, and in imminent danger of being shot. But no time was to be lost. As a subterfuge, one of the young men, a drover, began talking in the kindest tone of voice, saying to the cow-boy: "Now hold on; we are all cowboys just off of trail, and have been out to see a little fun. We have no money with us, but if you will just go with me to the Cottage, you shall have all the ten dollar notes you want. Certainly, certainly, sir! anything you want you can have, if you will only go with me to the hotel. Certainly, certainly, sir!"

Whilst this was being played, each of the other boys betook himself to his hands and knees and crawled away in the darkness until a few paces were gained, then tried his utmost capacity in running to a place of safety. In the meantime the cow-boy followed the spokesman, swearing instant death to every one if the money was not forthcoming. No sooner did they reach the Cottage than the young drover, after reassuring the cow-boy of his intention to get him the money, passed inside the hotel, and at once rushed for his pistols. But friends, who comprehended his intent and seeing "shoot in his eye," prevented him from going outside again. The cow-boy having his suspicions aroused by the delay, whirled his pony and dashed off for the village, screeching and yelling in genuine Indian style as he went. Coming to a large, open fronted tent, he dashed toward it, emptying the last loaded chamber of his revolver into it; then drawing his huge knife, cut the tent from end to end, and when it had fallen to the ground at his feet, rushed his pony over it, and was off for a bagnio, where he robbed every inmate of their money, jewelry and other valuables; then turned his pony's head toward the cattle trail and was off for Texas.

Such hard cases made it necessary to institute corporate government in the village. It was a hard struggle before law and order was established, and to maintain it cost the utmost firmness and perpetual vigilance. It was often necessary to disarm drunken cow-boys and such roughs as inevitably congregate at frontier commercial centers, which could be done only by force and terror. No quiet turned man could or would care to take the office of marshal, which jeopardized his life; hence the necessity of employing a desperado, one who feared nothing, and would as soon shoot an offending subject as to look at him.

The life of the cow-boy in camp is routine and dull. His food is largely of the "regulation" order, but a feast of vegetables he wants and must have, or scurvy would ensue. Onions and potatoes are his favorites, but any kind of vegetables will disappear in haste when put within his reach. In camp, on the trail, on the ranch in Texas, with their countless thousands of cattle, milk and butter are almost unknown, not even milk or cream for the coffee is had. Pure shiftlessness and the lack of energy are the only reasons for this privation, and to the same reasons can be assigned much of the privations and hardships incident to ranching.

It would cost but little effort or expense to add a hundred comforts, not to say luxuries, to the life of a drover and his cow-boys. They sleep on the ground, with a pair of blankets for bed and cover. No tent is used, scarcely any cooking utensils, and such a thing as a camp cook-stove is unknown. The warm water of the branch or the standing pool is drank; often it is yellow with alkali and other poisons. No wonder the cow-boy gets sallow and unhealthy, and deteriorates in manhood until often he becomes capable of any contemptible thing; no wonder he should become half-civilized only, and take to whisky with a love excelled scarcely by the barbarous Indian.

When the herd is sold and delivered to the purchaser, a day of rejoicing to the cow-boy has come, for then he can go free and have a jolly time; and it is a jolly time they have. Straightway after settling with their employers the barber shop is visited, and three to six months' growth of hair is shorn off, their long-grown, sunburnt beard "set" in due shape, and properly blacked; next a clothing store of the Israelitish style is "gone through," and the cow-boy emerges a new man, in outward appearance, everything being new, not excepting the hat and boots, with star decorations about the tops, also a new——, well in short everything new. Then for fun and frolic. The bar-room, the theatre, the gambling-room, the bawdy house, the dance house, each and all come in for their full share of attention. In any of these places an affront, or a slight, real or imaginary, is cause sufficient for him to unlimber one or more "mountain howitzers," invariably found strapped to his person, and proceed to deal out death in unbroken doses to such as may be in range of his pistols, whether real friends or enemies, no matter, his anger and bad whisky urge him on to deeds of blood and death.

At frontier towns where are centered many cattle and, as a natural result, considerable business is transacted, and many strangers congregate, there are always to be found a number of bad characters, both male and female; of the very worst class in the universe, such as have fallen below the level of the lowest type of the brute creation. Men who live a soulless, aimless life, dependent upon the turn of a card for the means of living. They wear out a purposeless life, ever looking blear-eyed and dissipated; to whom life, from various causes, has long since become worse than a total blank; beings in the form of man whose outward appearance would betoken gentlemen, but whose heart-strings are but a wisp of base sounding chords, upon which the touch of the higher and purer life have long since ceased to be felt. Beings without whom the world would be better, richer and more desirable. And with them are always found their counterparts in the opposite sex; those who have fallen low, alas! how low! They, too, are found in the frontier cattle town; and that institution known in the west as a dance house, is there found also. When the darkness of the night is come to shroud their orgies from public gaze, these miserable beings gather into the halls of the dance house, and "trip the fantastic toe" to wretched music, ground out of dilapidated instruments, by beings fully as degraded as the most vile. In this vortex of dissipation the average cow-boy plunges with great delight. Few more wild, reckless scenes of abandoned debauchery can be seen on the civilized earth, than a dance house in full blast in one of the many frontier towns. To say they dance wildly or in an abandoned manner is putting it mild. Their manner of practising the terpsichorean art would put the French "Can-Can" to shame.

The cow-boy enters the dance with a peculiar zest, not stopping to divest himself of his sombrero, spurs, or pistols, but just as he dismounts off of his cow-pony, so he goes into the dance. A more odd, not to say comical sight, is not often seen than the dancing cowboy; with the front of his sombrero lifted at an angle of fully forty-five degrees; his huge spurs jingling at every step or motion; his revolvers flapping up and down like a retreating sheep's tail; his eyes lit up with excitement, liquor and lust; he plunges in and "hoes it down" at a terrible rate, in the most approved yet awkward country style; often swinging "his partner" clear off of the floor for an entire circle, then "balance all" with an occasional demoniacal yell, near akin to the war whoop of the savage Indian. All this he does, entirely oblivious to the whole world "and the balance of mankind." After dancing furiously, the entire "set" is called to "waltz to the bar," where the boy is required to treat his partner, and, of course, himself also, which he does not hesitate to do time and again, although it costs him fifty cents each time. Yet if it cost ten times that amount he would not hesitate, but the more he dances and drink, the less common sense he will have, and the more completely his animal passions will control him. Such is the manner in which the cow-boy spends his hard earned dollars. And such is the entertainment that many young men—from the North and the South, of superior parentage and youthful advantages in life—give themselves up to, and often more, their lives are made to pay the forfeit of their sinful foolishness.

After a few days of frolic and debauchery, the cow-boy is ready, in company with his comrades, to start back to Texas, often not having one dollar left of his summer's wages. To this rather hard drawn picture of the cow-boy, there are many creditable exceptions, —young men who respect themselves and save their money, and are worthy young gentlemen,—but it is idle to deny the fact that the wild, reckless conduct of the cow-boys while drunk, in connection with that of the worthless northern renegades, have brought the *personnel* of the Texan cattle trade into great disrepute, and filled many graves with victims, bad men and good men, at Abilene, Newton, Wichita, and Ellsworth. But by far the larger portion of those killed are of that class that can be spared without detriment to the good morals and respectability of humanity.

It often occurs when the cow-boys fail to get up a melee and kill each other by the half dozen, that the keepers of those "hell's half acres" find some pretext arising from "business jealousies" or other causes, to suddenly become belligerent, and stop not to declare war, but begin hostilities at once. It is generally effective work they do with their revolvers and shot guns, for they are the most desperate men on earth. Either some of the principals or their subordinates are generally "done for" in a thorough manner, or wounded so as to be miserable cripples for life. On such occasions there are few tears shed, or even inquiries made, by the respectable people, but an expression of sorrow is common that, active hostilities did not continue until every rough was stone dead.

Richard Irving Dodge

"The most reckless of all the reckless desperadoes"

1882

Richard Irving Dodge presented his assessment of the cowboy in *Our Wild Indians: Thirty-three Years' Personal Experience Among the Red Men of the Great West*. A military man and one-time aide to General William Tecumseh Sherman, Dodge came to a discussion of the cowboy by way of a rhetorical investigation into the causes of Indian unrest in the West. Unsavory frontiersmen aggravated the Indians, he concluded, and among these rude folk were miners, buffalo hunters, and cowboys. His is the soldier's view.

Years ago, while yet a cherished portion of Mexico, Texas was famous for its cattle. Individuals owned thousands, even tens of thousands, which roamed almost at will, over the vast and fertile plains. The care of these was left to a few men and a crowd of Mexican boys from eight to twenty years of age; for not much money could be paid in wages, when the finest cow or fattest ox was worth but two or three dollars.

After the annexation of Texas to the United States the earlier drives of great herds of cattle were accompanied by such numbers of these boys, that all the herders were commonly called "Texas Cow-boys"; and though the cattle business has now spread over the greater portion of the great West; though the price of cattle has

From Richard Irving Dodge, *Our Wild Indians: Thirty-three Years' Personal Experience Among the Red Men of the Great West* (Hartford, A. D. Worthington & Co., 1882), 609–18.

increased so enormously that the best wages are given; and though the Mexican boys are replaced by full-grown white men, the appellative "cow-boy" is everywhere "out west" commonly applied to all those who herd cattle.

The daily life of the cow-boy is so replete with privation, hardship and danger, that it is a marvel how any sane man can voluntarily assume it, yet thousands of men not only do assume it, but actually like it to infatuation.

I doubt if there be in the whole world a class of men who lead lives so solitary, so exposed to constant hardship and danger, as this.

A large herd of cattle will be guarded by a number of men, who have a common place for eating and sleeping, but they are never there together. Day and night, in good weather and bad weather, some of them must be with the herd. The men are divided up into reliefs, each relief being on duty in the saddle not less than eight hours of the twenty-four, and each individual having a specified beat sometimes eight or ten miles long. Each relief must go around the whole herd, see that all are quiet and unmolested. The outside limits are carefully watched, and if any animals have strayed beyond them, their trail must be followed up, and the fugitives driven back to their proper grazing ground. Under ordinary circumstances, and when the herd is simply being held on certain good grazing ground, with abundance of water, these duties are comparatively easy; but when the grass is poor, and water scarce, the animals stray continually, and great watchfulness and labor are required for their care.

Especially is this the case in winter, when the grass is covered with snow. Cattle in large herds are easily stampeded, becoming panic-stricken on very slight, and frequently without, provocation. Nothing so starts them as a Plains "Norther," and they will fly before a severe storm of wind and snow sometimes for incredible distances. These are the trying times for the cow-boys. When a stampede occurs from any cause, every man must be in the saddle, follow the fleeing animals day and night, get control of the herd and bring it back to its ground. The worse the weather, the worse the stampede, and the greater the necessity for the presence and activity of the cow-boys.

A terrible Norther, during the winter of 1880, stampeded many herds in Southern Kansas and the Cherokee strip, some of which made fully ninety miles to the south before being got under control. With and among them were numbers of cow-boys, with only the scantiest ration of bread and meat, with no shelter or bedding, with no protection from the terrible cold except the clothing they happened to have on when the stampede was announced.

For fidelity to duty, for promptness and vigor of action, for resources in difficulty, and unshaken courage in danger, the cow-boy has no superior among men.

But there is something in this peculiar life which develops not only the highest virtues, but the most ignoble of vices. It is not solitude, for the shepherds of the Plains lead lives quite as solitary, and they are generally quiet, inoffensive persons. The cow-boy, on the contrary, is usually the most reckless of all the reckless desperadoes developed on the frontier. Disregarding equally the rights and lives of others, and utterly reckless of his own life; always ready with his weapons and spoiling for a fight, he is the terror of all who come near him, his visits to the frontier towns of Kansas and Nebraska being regarded as a calamity second only to a western tornado. His idea of enjoyment is to fill himself full of bad whiskey, mount his mustang, tear through the streets, whooping, yelling, flourishing and firing his pistols until the streets are deserted and every house closed, then with a grim smile of happiness he dashes off to his comrades to excite their envy by graphic pictures of his own exploits and the terror of the timid townspeople.

Cattle-stealing is a mania not confined solely to our Scotch ancestors. The frontier has many "cow-boys" out of employ, many impecunious gentlemen who long yearningly for a herd of cattle. The "waifs and strays" of large herds, or even a considerable herd, carelessly guarded, will suddenly disappear. Sometimes the herdsmen and the cattle disappear together, and should the owner be absent, are likely to disappear for him for all time.

In 1872 the owner of a considerable herd returned to his ranche in Southeastern Kansas after a short absence, to find his herd and herders gone. Taking the trail alone, he plodded west for more than one hundred miles, when he found about half his herd in the possession of a notorious desperado near where Larned City now stands. On inquiry he found they had recently been *purchased* of a man who had gone still further west with the other half. Following on, he found his herd in charge of its reputed owner on the Arkansas River near Fort Dodge. The thief was the most notoriously blood-thirsty ruffian on the frontier. After a terrible combat the thief was killed, and the owner, collecting his cattle, returned with them eastward. Arriving at the ranche of the robber who had his others, he went to him and said quietly, "I have taken the scalp of your partner and got half my cattle. I want to know if I'll have to take your scalp to get the other half." The terrified ruffian gave them up without a contest.

A few years ago the beef contractor at one of the military posts in the Indian Territory had an adventure which I will let him tell in his own idiom.

"Wall, boys, I was mighty nigh onto busted that time, an' I'll tell you about it. You see I'd worked hard an' roughed it, an' got a nice little lot of cattle. The contract for this post was to be let, I bid on it, an' got it. Wall, my cattle was none of the best, the grass was poor, an' afore long the commandin' officer says to me, says he, 'There's complaints agin your beef, you must do better, or I will order the commissary to buy good beef and charge it to yer.' Says I, 'Commandin' officer, I know my beef is none of the best, but give me a little time, and I'll get yer the very best.' 'All right,' says he, 'but do it.' So next mornin' I put some money in my belt and started for Texas. I bought a hundred and fifty head of first class beef, and hired a Mexican boy to help me drive 'em. He was only a little chap about twelve years old, but he was powerful bright and handy, and, sand! lots! I had a breech-loadin' rifle, and pistols, but the Injuns was bad, so I bought a double-barrelled shotgun for the boy. Every-thing went on all right till we'd got into the territory about one hundred miles from here. One mornin' we was movin' along, when a man rode up to me. He was a small-sized man, but the handsomest man I ever seed, an' dressed the handsomest. He had on high boots, big silver spurs, an' buckskin breeches, an' a buckskin huntin'-shirt all over fringes, an' open at the front. He had on a white biled shirt, an' a red silk necktie with long ends a flyin' behind. Around his waist was a red silk sash, an' he wore a regular Mexican sombrero, an' his bridle an' saddle was Mexican, an' covered with silver. He was on a splendid mustang that bucked an' shied all the time, but he rode him like his skin. I tell you, boys, it was a handsome outfit. 'Good mornin',' says he, a liftin' up his hat mighty polite. 'Good mornin',' says I, an' with that we chatted along pleasant like. He told me that he had a big herd of cattle about three miles to the east, an' he was afraid I'd give 'em the fever, an' he wanted me to keep more to the left, off his range. Wall, I was agreeable, an' he kept with me for a mile an' more, showin' me where to go and then thankin' me polite, he said good-bye, an' rode off. Wall now, boys, I had kept on the course he told me for about two hours, when just beyant a little rise I drove right into my gentleman friend an' six other fellers. Ridin' right up to me, my friend says, says he, 'after thinkin' it over, I have concluded it would be a pity to lose such a extra fine lot of beef cattle as you have got, so I have concluded to take 'em in.' Wall, boys, I saw right through the thing in a minit. I knowed it were no use to fight agin so many, so I begged. I told him how I was situate, that if I didn't get them cattle to the post I was ruinated. He listened for a few minutes pretty quiet, an' I thot I had got him, when all at once he drawed a pistol, an' all the other fellers drawed their pistols at the same time.

" 'My friend,' says he, 'we don't take no advantage of cattle-men, but them cattle of yours is the same as Government property. They is going to feed soldiers. All such property is as much ours as anybody's, now you git'—and with that he stuck his cocked pistol in my face, an' all the other six stuck their cocked pistols at me. Wall, boys, me and that Mexican boy—we left.

"Them fellers rounded up my cattle, an' drove 'em back ther own way. Boys, my heart was most broke. I knowed I was ruinated if I lost them cattle. Wall, we travelled along for a mile or more, when I made up my mind. 'Domingo,' says I to the little Mexican, 'are you afeared to stay and take care of the hosses, while I settle with them chaps?' 'No,' says he, 'an' I'll help you ef you want me.'

"The country was about half prairie, an' t'other half the thickest kind of black jack, and scrub-oak thickets. I hid that boy an' them hosses wher a hound couldn't ev found 'em, and when it got towards evenin', I started on foot to hunt up my friends' cattle camp, an' as I knowed I had to get in my work in the dark an' at close range, I took the boy's double-barrel shot-gun, each barrel loaded with sixteen buckshot, an' big size at that.

"About midnight I found the herd. The cattle was held in a prairie with thickets all around it. I poked around, keepin' in the thickets. They had about a thousand head not countin' mine. I found ther 'dug out.' Ther was two men on herd. I poked around till I found wher my cattle was. They knowed me, an didn't make no fuss when I went among 'em. Thar I laid down in the grass. In about an hour one of the herders rode right close on to me, an' I let him have one barrel. In a minit the other herder hollered out, 'what the h—l is that,' an' gettin no answer he galloped right over ther, and I give him the other barrel. I got back to the thicket and went to my camp, an' to sleep. Next mornin' when the sun was way up, that boy he woke me, an' says, says he, 'ther havin a high time in that camp, you had better be looking after 'em.' Wall, I got my breakfast an went to look after 'em. They wus in a big commotion, all of 'em together, huntin' everywhere for my trail. I had wored mocassins, an' I knowed none of 'em fellows could follow my trail. I had another big advantage of 'em. They couldn't go nowhere unless they wus on hossback, and the brush wus so thick they had to ride in the open prairie whar I could see 'em. I poked round in the thicket wher they couldn't see me. Next night I tried it agin, but they wus all on herd and held the cattle out in the prairie so fur from the woods that I had no show. I changed my plan, an' went back to my camp. Next mornin' I was out early pokin' in the thickets and watchin'. A lot of cattle grazed up towards a pint of woods. I knowed they would stop that soon, so I hid in that pint. Pretty soon a feller came chargin' round on a full run after them cattle. He was a likely chap, an' I felt a little oneasy until I recognized him as having stuck a pistol in my face two days before. I got him.

"Wall, boys, thar's no use in stringin' this thing out. Them chaps wus scared from the start, and would have got out of thar, if they hadn't had to go through thickets. I knowed that, an' took it easy. In three days I had gradually got away with them. They wus so few that they couldn't herd ther cattle. On the mornin' of the fourth day I noticed a lot of cattle feedin' off. They wus nigh two miles from the dug-out—I laid with 'em, but in the thicket. Towards afternoon a feller came dashin' in at full speed an' rounded up within twenty feet of me. When he fell he was so tied up in his lariat that he stopped the hoss. I caught an' tied that hoss in a thicket, so that the others at the dug-out wouldn't know this man was dead.

After the second day I had never seed my fine captain. He had made the others take chances, but he had stayed in the dug-out, an' run no risk himself. I thought if I could get him I'd be all right. So, afore day next mornin' I hid in a break about twenty yards from the door of the dug-out, an just at daybreak I covered that door with my shot-gun, an' fired off my pistol with the other hand. As I expected, he jumped out of the door with his gun in his hand, but he had no chance an' no time, I doubled him up right in the door. In a few minits a white rag was stuck out of the door on a stick. I called to the man to come out, and put up his hands, an' he did. I walked up an' said to him, 'I ought to kill you, but I won't if you will do as I tell yer. Get your hoss, cut out my cattle, and drive 'em over to that hill.' He said, says he, 'I never saw you before, an' I don't know your cattle; I am the cook of this outfit, an' I am the only man left.' So I made him get me a hoss, an' he an me cut out my cattle, an' drove 'em over near my camp, an' me an' the boy took 'em, and by hard drivin' got to the post in time. It were a tight fit, boys; an' now, what'll yer have to drink."

To the miners and the cow-boys we owe most of our complications with Indians. The one class in search of the precious metals; the other in search of good grazing grounds; the one over-running the mountains, the other pre-empting the plains and valleys; all, careless of the rights, and impatient of the claims, of Indians; all, with a ferocity begot of greed, hating the Indian, hating a Government which, they believe, protects and perpetually pauperizes the Indian at their expense; all ready and willing to bring on any conflict between the Government and the Indian, which may lessen the numbers and diminish the Territory of the latter; they go anywhere and everywhere, constantly pushing the Indian to the wall, constantly forcing issues suited to their own ends; constantly showing the inadequacy of the laws and forces of a popular government to the enforcement of unpopular measures, and rendering futile and ridiculous all treaties made with Indians.

Walter Baron von Richthofen

"Among cowboys are to be found the sons of the best families"

1885

Walter Baron von Richthofen emigrated from Germany to Colorado in the mid-1870's, became involved in several business ventures there, and lived a life of luxury and leisure in Denver. He owned some dairy cattle, and that apparently was the extent of his involvement with stock raising. He learned what he knew of the range-cattle industry from friends. His book, *Cattle-Raising on the Plains of North America*, first published in 1885, was a promotional piece, and his commentary on the cowboy is interesting because it was designed to be read by potential investors in American beef. (The name is indeed the same. Von Richthofen's nephew was Germany's famed Red Baron of World War I.)

Terms used in the cattle business are not generally known East and abroad, and I will therefore give their definition, as I shall have to use them repeatedly in the following chapters.

The owners of cattle in the Western stock-raising states are required by law to brand their stock with initials, figures, etc., chosen by themselves. The iron brands are attached to long handles, and pressed, when red-hot, upon one or the other side, or both sides, on especially selected parts of the animal, and thereby are written unmistakable and everlasting marks.

By law every brand must be registered in the office of the

From Walter Baron von Richthofen, *Cattle-Raising on the Plains of North America* (intro. by Edward Everett Dale, Norman, University of Oklahoma Press, new ed., 1964), 16–22, 27–30. Reprinted by permission of the publisher.

counties in which herds are expected to graze, and it is the duty of the recording clerk to see that a newcomer does not select an already registered brand. In the change of ownership of cattle, the seller brands the animal with his "vend" brand, which is the proof for the buyer of his title, and the buyer puts his brand on in addition. The brand proves, therefore, the ownership or title to the animal.

Heretofore cattle have been caught by lassos and then branded. Of late, grown cattle have been driven into narrow shoots of varied lengths, and made to stand one behind the other, so close that they can hardly move, and the man through the openings between the timbers of the shoot impresses the brand.

Lassoing requires much practice, and is the great pleasure as well as the essential accomplishment of a good herder or cowboy.

Among cowboys are to be found the sons of the best families, who enjoy this romantic, healthy, and free life on the prairie.

Good opportunities to watch the skill of these cowboys are offered during round-ups, which is to the spectator a very interesting scene.

As the word shows, it is a rounding up and driving together of all the cattle within given limits to one selected spot. Naturally this work is performed on horseback, and every owner of cattle within the district, with his herders, takes part therein.

The purpose of a round-up is the following: As herds spread over considerable territory, it would be a great sacrifice of time, money, and labor if single owners of herds had to hunt up singly their cattle in order to sell or to brand the same. For that reason the owners cooperate and drive all the cattle within their district together, make their bargains, brand their calves and steers, and complete the stock books of their herds, which owners are required by law to keep.

Between the middle of April and the end of June each year a general round-up is made, in which all herd-owners participate. Its principal purpose is the branding of the increase. In the months of September and October there are smaller round-ups, organized by those herd-owners who wish to collect fat steers for the market; but branding is also done.

Every Western state in which the industry of cattle-raising is important has its stock laws, the most important of which I will mention in an early chapter.

Every state government has subdivided its state into round-up districts, which vary in size between 100 and 150 square miles, according to the topography of the country. The governor of each state appoints a commission of three herd-owners in each district, called round-up commissioners, whose duty it is to see that the so-called round-up laws are executed; to make the programme for the general round-up; to fix the day of beginning, and subdivide their districts into smaller districts, averaging 10 to 12 square miles, which can be rounded up in a day, to publish in all papers the programme of the round-up, and appoint a captain as head of the practical execution of the same.

The captain is generally an experienced small herd-owner, who is thoroughly acquainted with the topography of his district, has an extensive knowledge of brands, and is familiar with the peculiarities of cattle.

From the beginning of the round-up he is the absolute commander.

On these days all the owners of cattle meet, attended with their herders, and well supplied with wagons, tents, blankets, provisions, and saddle horses.

The horses have the hardest work during the round-up, and are not expected to be used longer than half a day. Every herder needs to have at least from three to five horses in reserve.

The horses best adapted for cattle business are those raised on the plains. They are very hardy, between fourteen and fifteen hands high, large boned, and ugly looking. They cost between forty and fifty dollars apiece.

On the first day of a general round-up the camp is established. Twenty or thirty tents are pitched, and soon the smoke rises and the charms of a vivid camp life are offered to the eyes of the spectators. Wagons in profusion stand about, and hobbled horses graze around. The captain makes his general dispositions for round-up. The herd-owners divide the different duties of the work among their herders—some to go on the round-up, some to do branding, and others to cut out the beeves which are to be sold and drive them to the nearest railroad station or market. The buyers and sellers exchange their opinions regarding the interests and future of the business, and often conclude bargains.

The next morning early the work begins. The captain collects his herders, and gives them their instructions where to ride, where to find the cattle, and where to drive them.

This spot, where all cattle within the day's district are to be driven together, has been previously selected by the captain. It is generally a place, not necessarily in the center of the district, where a large herd of cattle can easily be controlled, and where there is grass and water enough for a large number of animals for several days.

After the herders have received their general instructions, they gallop off right and left, while the owners, buyers, and ever-present spectators move toward the place where the large herd will be rounded up.

In a few hours one can note scattered groups of cattle approaching, followed by larger masses, until the herders themselves bring up, with yell and halloo, the refractory and more stubborn animals. Toward noon from two to five thousand head of cattle are collected. It is by no means an easy task to quiet so large a herd. It generally takes an hour or two for the different groups of strange cattle to learn to tolerate each other's presence, and to establish quiet among the steers, many of which make frequent attempts to break through the chain of herders, which is kept up around the herd day and night, like a cordon of sentries. At last one can see how the larger and stronger steers, seeking the center of the herd, resign themselves to their fate, and how the careful mother-cow keeps her calf on the outside, away from the danger of being trampled down or hurt by its older and untamed brothers and cousins.

Now begins the work of branding the calves.

The cowboy rides into the herd, cuts out a cow with an unbranded calf, throws his well-directed lasso, catches and jerks the calf to the ground, which another herder quickly brands and releases from the lasso; and then they seek out another victim. Some of the herd-owners collect all their cows and calves in a bunch, drive them to their home ranches, and do the branding there after the general round-up is over.

If sales of grown cattle are made, the buyer brands his purchases on the spot, lassoing them as above described, which is very hard work. If a great number are to be branded, branding-pens must be constructed, or the cattle driven to the home ranch. As stated before, owners of herds can now count their cattle.

As evening approaches it is very difficult to keep a herd together, but at night the cattle generally lie down and sleep. The work is resumed the next day, and continued from day to day until all the calves or grown cattle are branded and all steers and barren cows intended for market are cut out and collected, when the rest of the herd are allowed to go free. These proceedings often occupy several days. The camp then breaks up and moves to another part of the district, where the same work is repeated, and so on until the whole district has been gone over. . . .

About noon herds move toward their watering places, where they remain for two or three hours, and then, like buffalo, march back in single file to their favorite pasture grounds. In summer they seldom graze farther than five or six miles from water, while in winter they spread over more territory, often remaining two or three days without water, and even eating snow for drink. During a heavy snow storm groups and families gather together into small herds, and, with their back to the storm, shelter one another. Long-continued snow storms drive such herds from their home pastures into other regions; but when the storm clears they generally return to their haunts. In northern climates, where snow storms are more frequent, cattle die from hunger only when they are so driven for shelter in large numbers to a place with natural barriers which stop them, and where they soon consume all the grass; but this very seldom happens. As a rule, cattle cling with instinctive love to the pastures which they have once occupied.

The duties of the herders may now be mentioned. From April to June, during the general round-up, herders have the hardest work of the year. From July to the end of August the herder, always on horseback, hunts in neighboring pastures for strayed cattle, drives them back to their own pastures, and brands such young calves as he may find. The finding of lost cattle is not as difficult as may at first appear, for the cattlemen are always on good terms with one another. When a herder arrives at a camp inquiring after lost stock, he invariably receives all information from willing friends and offers of

assistance. Herders when on the hunt for lost cattle are never allowed to pay for their lodgings overnight, and, should one of their
horses be tired out or lame, they always are offered another without
charge.

September and October are the months for private round-ups
for the purpose of collecting beef for the market, and for branding
any calves that may have escaped. Unbranded calves, if found with
their mothers, even though they may not belong to the parties interested in these fall round-ups, are branded for their real owners,
and a registry kept and forwarded to those interested. This latter
work, which is not paid for, but is a matter of honor, proves how
herd-owners help one another.

The labor in November and December is much the same as in
midsummer, only perhaps more with the view of finding lost fat-beef
cattle for market. Between January and April there is very little work
to be done. During that time the cattle get rest and are not molested
by being constantly driven. According to the resolutions of the association of cattle-growers, no calf may be branded during this time.
All that the herders are then expected to do is to keep a general
supervision of the stock, and after snow storms to drive lost stock
back to their ranges. During the whole year the herders have many
different jobs to perform on their home ranches, such as cooking,
cutting wood, hay-making, etc.

The following statement shows how many herders are necessary for the management of a herd of five thousand head, and the
cost of their pay and sustenance:

A good foreman engaged by the year is indispensable. His
salary may be from $60 to $70 per month, with free lodging and
board, valued at about $20 per month. From the first of April to the
first of July seven herders are necessary, each at a salary of $35 per
month and board. From the first of July to the first of December only
five herders are needed, and from that time until the first of April
the foreman with one herder can do all the work. The wages for the
whole year would amount to $2,580, and board would cost $1,120.
Total $3,700 per annum. The estimate of the cost of board may be
too high; $3,500 per annum would probably be ample. From this we
see that the cost of labor in herding five thousand head is seventy

cents per head per annum. To keep one thousand head more would cost but a trifle addition.

The equipment for every herder consists of from three to five ponies, a first-class Mexican saddle, lasso, etc. I have already described the kind of horses which are used. They are never fed with grain, but have to find their own food like the cattle. Their only training is in accustoming them to the saddle and the throwing of the lasso, in which they play the most important part. In former years owners of small bunches of cattle hired the herding of their stock for a percentage of the increase, or paid one dollar per head per annum. This is seldom done now, and only in cases where owners can not devote their whole time and attention to their cattle.

Charles A. Siringo

"I spent my last dime for a glass of lemonade"

1885

It was inevitable that eventually the cowboy would begin to speak for himself. In 1885, Charlie Siringo published his autobiography, *A Texas Cow Boy or, Fifteen Years on the Hurricane Deck of a Spanish Pony*, the first of many cowboy memoirs. Siringo had no lofty purpose in mind when he set pen to paper. He wrote, he admitted in unabashed candor, to make money. Countless others followed his example. Siringo's book appeared in many editions between 1885 and 1926.

I put in the following winter branding Mavricks, skinning cattle and making regular trips to Matagorda; I still remained in partnership with Horace Yeamans in the skinning business. I made considerable money that winter as I sold a greater number of Mavricks than ever before. But the money did me no good as I spent it freely.

That coming spring, it being 1874, I hired to Leander Ward of Jackson county to help gather a herd of steers for the Muckleroy Bros., who were going to drive them to Kansas. I had also made a contract with Muckleroy's boss, Tom Merril, to go up the trail with him, therefore I bid my friends good-bye, not expecting to see them again until the coming fall. My wages were thirty-five dollars per month and all expenses, including railroad fare back home.

From Charles A. Siringo, *A Texas Cow Boy or, Fifteen Years on the Hurricane Deck of a Spanish Pony* (Chicago, Rand, McNally & Co., 1886), 95–102, 176–85, 337–40.

After a month's hard work we had the eleven hundred head of wild and woolly steers ready to turn over to the Muckleroy outfit at Thirteen mile point on the Mustang, where they were camped, ready to receive them. Their outfit consisted mostly of Kansas "short horns" which they had brought back with them the year before.

It was a cold, rainy evening when the cattle were counted and turned over to Tom Merril. Henry Coats, Geo. Gifford and myself were the only boys who were turned over with the herd—that is kept right on. We were almost worn out standing night guard half of every night for the past month and then starting in with a fresh outfit made it appear tough to us.

That night it began to storm terribly. The herd began to drift early and by midnight we were five or six miles from camp. The steers showed a disposition to stampede but we handled them easy and sang melodious songs which kept them quieted. But about one o'clock they stampeded in grand shape. One of the "short horns," a long legged fellow by the name of Saint Clair got lost from the herd and finally when he heard the singing came dashing through the herd at full speed yelling "let 'em slide, we'll stay with'em!" at every jump.

They did slide sure enough, but he failed to "stay with 'em." For towards morning one of the boys came across him lying in the grass sound asleep. When he came dashing through the herd a stampede followed; the herd split up into a dozen different bunches— each bunch going in a different direction. I found myself all alone with about three hundred of the frightened steers. Of course all I could do was to keep in front or in the lead and try to check them up. I finally about three o'clock got them stopped and after singing a few "lullaby" songs they all lay down and went to snoring.

After the last steer dropped down I concluded I would take a little nap too, so locking both legs around the saddle-horn and lying over on the tired pony's rump, with my left arm for a pillow, while the other still held the bridle-reins, I fell asleep. I hadn't slept long though when, from some unaccountable reason, every steer jumped to his feet at the same instant and was off like a flash. My pony which was sound asleep too, I suppose, became frightened and dashed off at full speed in the opposite direction. Of course I was also frightened and hung to the saddle with a death grip. I was unable to raise myself up as the pony was going so fast, therefore had to remain as I was, until after about a mile's run I got him checked up.

Just as soon as I got over my scare I struck out in a gallop in the direction I thought the cattle had gone, but failed to overtake them. I landed in camp almost peetered out about nine o'clock next morning. The rest of the boys were all there, just eating their breakfast. Tom Merril and Henry Coats had managed to hold about half of the herd, while the balance were scattered and mixed up with "range" cattle for twenty miles around.

After eating our breakfast and mounting fresh horses we struck out to gather up the lost steers. We could tell them from the range cattle by the fresh "road" brand—a brand that had been put on a few days before—therefore, by four o'clock that evening we had all but about one hundred head back to camp and those Leander Ward bought back at half price—that is he just bought the road brand or all cattle that happened to be left behind.

On arriving at camp, we all caught fresh horses before stopping to eat dinner or supper, whichever you like to call it, it being then nearly night. The pony I caught was a wild one and after riding up to camp and dismounting to eat dinner, he jerked loose from me and went a flying with my star-spangled saddle.

I mounted a pony belonging to one of the other boys and went in hot pursuit. I got near enough once to throw my rope over his rump and that was all. After a run of fifteen miles I gave it up as a bad job and left him still headed for the Rio Grande.

I got back to camp just at dark and caught a fresh horse before stopping to eat my supper. It was still raining and had kept it up all day long. Mr. "Jim" Muckleroy had an extra saddle along therefore I borrowed it until I could get a chance to buy me another one.

After eating a cold supper, the rain having put the fire out, I mounted and went on "guard," the first part of the night, until one o'clock, being my regular time to stay with the herd, while the last "guard" remained in camp and slept.

About ten o'clock it began to thunder and lightning, which caused the herd to become unruly. Every time a keen clash of thunder would come the herd would stampede and run for a mile or two before we could get them to stop. It continued in that way all night so that we lost another night's rest; but we managed to "stay with 'em" this time; didn't even loose a steer.

That morning we struck out on the trail for Kansas. Everything went on smoothly with the exception of a stampede now and then and a fuss with Jim Muckleroy, who was a regular old sore-head. Charlie, his brother was a white man. Where the trouble began, he wanted Coats and I, we being the only ones in the crowd who could ride wild horses—or at least who were willing to do so, to do the wild horse riding for nothing. We finally bolted and told him that we wouldn't ride another wild horse except our regular "mount," unless he gave us extra pay. You see he expected us to ride a horse a few times until he began to get docile and then turn him over to one of his muley pets while we caught up a fresh one.

At High Hill in Fayette county I got the bounce from old Jim and a little further on Coats got the same kind of a dose; while nearing the northern state-line Geo. Gifford and Tom Merril, the boss, were fired; so that left old Jim in full charge. He hired other men in our places. He arrived in Wichita, Kansas with eight hundred steers, out of the eleven hundred we started with.

After leaving the outfit I rode to the Sunset railroad at Shuzenburg and boarded a train for Columbus on the Colorado river. "Pat" Muckleroy, Charlie's son, who was about eighteen years old, quit and went with me. His home was in Columbus and he persuaded me to accompany him and have a good time.

On arriving in Columbus I went with Pat to his home where I remained during my stay in that place. I found Mrs. M., Pat's mother, to be a kind-hearted old lady, and I never shall forget the big, fat apple cobblers she used to make; she could beat the world making them. There were also two young Misses in the family, Nannie and Mary, who made time pass off pleasantly with me.

It being seventy-five miles to Tresspalacious and there being no railroad nearer than that, I had to wait for a chance to get home. I could have bought a horse and saddle when I first struck town but after remaining there a week I began to get light in the pocket, for it required quite a lot of money to keep up my end with the crowd that Pat associated with.

At last after about a three weeks stay, I struck Asa Dawdy, an old friend from Tresspalacious. He was there with a load of stock and was just fixing to load them on the cars to ship them to Galveston when I ran afoul of him. He had sold his saddle and was going to put his pet pony, one that he wouldn't sell, into a pasture until some other time when he happened up there. So you see I was in luck; he turned the pony over to me to ride home on.

After buying and rigging up a saddle I left town flat broke. I spent my last dime for a glass of lemonade just before leaving. Thus ended my first experience on the "trail." . . .

After laying around the ranch a couple of weeks, Mr. Moore put me in charge of a scouting outfit and sent me out on the South Plains to drift about all winter, watching for cattle thieves, etc.; also to turn back any cattle that might slip by the "sign riders" and drift across the Plains.

During that winter we, that is my crowd, went to church several times. A little Colony of Christians headed by the Rev. Cahart, had settled on the head of Salt Fork, a tributary of Red river, and built a church house in which the little crowd, numbering less than fifty souls would congregate every Sunday and pray.

That same little church house now ornaments the thriving little city of Clarendon, County seat of Donley County. The old inhabitants point to it with pride when telling of how it once stood solitary and alone out on the great buffalo range two hundred miles from nowhere.

The Colony had come from Illinois and drifted away out there beyond the outskirts of civilization to get loose from that demon, whisky. And early that coming spring a lot of ruffians started a saloon in their midst. A meeting was called in the little church house and resolutions passed to drive them out, if in no other way, with powder and lead. They pulled their freight and I am proud to state that I had a hand in making them pull it; for the simple reason that they had no business encroaching upon those good people's rights.

When spring opened Mr. Moore called me in from the Plains and put me in charge of a rounding-up outfit, which consisted of twelve riders and a cook.

To begin rounding-up, we went over to Canyon Paladuro, where Chas. Goodnight had a ranch, and where a great many of the river cattle had drifted during the winter. There was about a hundred men and seven or eight wagons in the outfit that went over. We stopped over Sunday in the little Christian Colony and went to church. The Rev. Cahart preached about the wild and woolly Cow Boy of the west; how the eastern people had him pictured off as a kind of animal with horns, etc. While to him, looking down from his dry goods box pulpit into the manly faces of nearly a hundred of them, they looked just like human beings, minus the standing collar.

About the first of July, Moore sent me to Nickerson, Kansas, with a herd of eight hundred shipping steers. My outfit consisted of five men, a chuck wagon, etc. Our route lay over a wild strip of country where there was no trails nor scarcely any ranches—that is, until reaching the southern line of Kansas.

We arrived at Nickerson after being on the road two months. "Deacon" Bates, Mr. Beals partner, was there waiting for us. He had come through with several herds that had left the ranch a month ahead of us. He was still holding some of the poorest ones, south of town, where he had a camp established.

After loading my wagon with a fresh supply of grub, Mr. Bates, or the "Deacon" as he was more commonly called, sent me back over the trail he and his outfits had come, to gather lost steers—some they had lost coming through.

I was gone about a month and came back with eighteen head. We had a soft trip of it, as most of our hard work was such as buying butter, eggs, etc., from the scattering grangers along the Kansas border. We never missed a meal on the trip, and always had the best the country afforded, regardless of cost. Deacon Bates was always bragging on some of his bosses, how cheap they could live, etc. I just thought I would try him this time, being in a country where luxuries were plentiful, and see if he wouldn't blow on me as being a person with good horse sense. An animal of course, as we all know, will eat the choicest grub he can get; and why not man, when he is credited with having more sense than the horse, one of the most intellectual animals that exists?

On our return to Nickerson, I concluded to quit and spend the winter with mother, whom I received letters from every now and then begging me to come home. As I wasn't certain of coming back, I thought it best to go overland and take Whisky-peet along, for I couldn't even bear the *thought* of parting with him; and to hire a car to take him around by rail would be too costly.

I got all ready to start and then went to Deacon Bates for a settlement. He took my account book and, after looking it over, said: "Why, Dum-it to h——l, I can't pay no such bills as those! Why, Dum-it all, old Jay Gould would groan under the weight of these bills!" He then went on to read some of the items aloud. They ran as follows: Cod-fish $10; eggs $40; butter $70; milk $5; bacon $150; flour $200; canned fruits $400; sundries $600, etc., etc. Suffice it to say, the old gent told me in plain Yankee English that I would have to go to Chicago and settle with Mr. Beals. I hated the idea of going to Chicago, for I knew my failings—I was afraid I wouldn't have money enough left when I got back to pay my expenses home.

That same evening a letter came from Mr. Beals stating that he had just received a letter from Moore, at the ranch, in which he informed him that there were two more herds on the trail for Nickerson, and, as it was getting so near winter, for Joe Hargraves, better known as "Jinglebob Joe," and I to go and turn them to Dodge City, the nearest shipping point.

After putting Whisky-peet and my "Missouri" mare, one I had bought to use as a pack-horse going home, in care of an old granger to be fed and taken good care of until my return, Joe and I struck out with only one horse apiece—just the ones we were riding.

On our arrival in Dodge I pulled out for Chicago, to get a settlement, with the first train load we shipped. I took my saddle, bridle, spurs, etc. along and left them in Atchison, Mo., the first point we stopped to feed at, until my return.

Arriving in Chicago, I told Mr. Beals that I was going home to spend the winter, and therefore wanted to settle up.

He set 'em up to a fine Havana and then proceeded. Every time he came to one of those big bills, which caused the Deacon's eyes to bulge out, he would grunt and crack about a forty-cent smile, but never kicked.

When he had finished there was a few hundred dollars to my credit. He then asked me if I could think of anything else that I had forgotten to charge the "company" with? Of course I couldn't, because I didn't have time; his question was put to me too sudden. If I could have had a few hours to myself, to figure the thing up just right, I think I could have satisfied the old Gent.

I remained in the city three days taking in the sights and feeding the hungry little boot blacks. When leaving, Mr. Beals informed me that he was going to buy a lot of southern Texas cattle, to put on his Panhandle ranch, the coming spring, and if I wanted a job, to hold myself in readiness to boss one of the herds up the trail for him. Of course that just suited me, providing I couldn't make up my mind to remain at home.

Landing in Nickerson I hired a horse and went out to the old granger's ranch where I had left my two ponies. They were both fat and feeling good.

Before starting out on my little journey of only eleven hundred miles, I bought a pack-saddle and cooking outfit—that is, just a frying pan, small coffee pot, etc. I used the mare for a pack animal and rode Whisky-peet. I had just six dollars left when I rode out of Nickerson.

I went through Fort Reno and Fort Sill, Indian territory and crossed Red river into Texas on the old military road, opposite Henrietta.

When within ten miles of Denton, Texas, on Pecan creek, Whisky-peet became lame—so much so that he could scarcely walk. I was stopping over night with a Mr. Cobb, and next morning I first noticed his lameness.

I lacked about twenty-five cents of having enough to pay Mr. Cobb for my night's lodging that morning. I had sold my watch for five dollars a short while before and now that was spent.

Whisky-peet being too lame to travel, I left him with Mr. Cobb while I rode into Denton to try and make a raise of some money.

I tried to swap my mare off for a smaller animal and get some boot, but every one seemed to think that she had been stolen; I being so anxious to swap.

I rode back to Mr. Cobb's that night in the same fix, financially, as when I left that morning.

The next day I made a raise of some money. Mr. Cobb and I made a saddle swap, he giving me twenty dollars to boot. He and I also swapped bridles, I getting four dollars and a half to boot. One of his little boys then gave me his saddle and one dollar and a half for my pack-saddle, which had cost me ten dollars in Nickerson. I then had lots of money.

Whisky-peet soon got over his lameness, having just stuck a

little snag into the frog of his foot, which I succeeded in finding and pulling out before it had time to do serious damage, and I started on my journey again.

On arriving in Denton that time, a negro struck me for a horse swap right away. I got a three year old pony and six dollars in money for my mare; the pony suited just as well for a pack animal as the mare.

The next day after leaving Denton, I stopped in a negro settlement and won a fifty-dollar horse, running Whisky-peet against a sleepy looking grey. I had up twenty dollars in money and my Winchester, a fine silver mounted gun. I won the race by at least ten open feet, but the negroes tried to swindle me out of it.

While riding along that evening three negroes rode up and claimed the horse I had won. They claimed that the parties who bet him off had no right to him, as they just had borrowed him from one of them to ride to the Settlement that morning. I finally let them have him for twenty dollars.

I went through the following towns after leaving Denton: Ft. Worth, Clenborn, Hillsborough, Waco, Herrene, Bryant, Brenham and Columbus; besides scores of smaller places.

I rode up to mother's little shanty on Cashe's creek after being on the road just a month and twelve days.

To say that mother was glad to see me would only half express it. She bounced me the first thing about not coming back the next fall after leaving as I had promised. I had been gone nearly four years. . . .

A cowboys outfit is something like a Boston dudes' rig, it can be bought for a small or large amount of money according to the purchasers' means and inclinations.

If you wish to put on style and at the same time have a serviceable outfit, you can invest $500.00 very handy; that is by going or sending to Texas or Old Mexico the only place where such costly outfits are kept.

Your saddle would cost $100. although the Mexicans have them as high as $300.00. An other $50.00 for a gold mounted Mexican sombraro (hat). And $100.00 for a silver mounted bridle and spurs to match. Now a $50.00 saddle-blanket to match your saddle and another $25.00 for a squirt and "Re-etta" (raw-hide rope). Your

Colts "45" pearl-handled gold mounted pistol would cost $50.00, a Winchester to match, $75.00 and $25.00 for a pair of Angora goat leggings, making a total of $475.00 leaving $25.00 out of the $500.00 to buy a Spanish buggy with.

Years ago costly outfits worn by nearly all Cow-men but this day and age are seldom indulged—the simple reason that now-days it requires more rough and tumble hard work than skill to command good wages on a cattle ranch. Cattle are becoming so tame from being bred up with short horns that it requires but very little skill and knowledge to be a Cow-boy. I believe the day is not far distant when cow-boys will be armed with prod-poles to punch the cattle out of their way—instead of fire-arms. Messrs Colt and Winchester will have to go out of business or else emigrate to Arkansas and open up prod-pole factories.

Well now for the cost of a common outfit, with a few words of advise to the young tender-foot who wishes to become a Cow-boy.

Mount a Railroad and go to any of the large "shipping" or "cattle-towns,"—then purchase a cheap pony, for about $25.00; saddle for $25.00; leather leggings for $5.00; broad-brim White-hat for $10.00; saddle-bags which would do to sleep on also 50.00. Another $5.00 bill for spurs, bridle, stake-rope etc.

And now for the most important ornament the old reliable "45" Pistol Colts, 12.00. If you are foolish enough to go without the latter, the cooks at the different ranches where you happen to stop will not respect you. Instead of putting the handle to you family name they will call you the sore-footed kid, Old-man Nibbs or some names as those. We know from experience that the pistol carries much weight with it, and therefore especially advise the young "tenderfoot" to buy one, even if he has to ride bare-backed, from not having money enough left to buy a saddle with.

Having your outfit all ready, the next thing to be done is, inquire the distance, north, south and west, to the nearest railroad from the town you are in. And which ever one is furthest, strike right out boldly for it. When you get about *half* way there, stop at the first ranch you come to, even if you have to work for your "chuck." The idea is to get just as far from a railroad as possible.

If you go to work for your "chuck," while doing so, work just as hard, and if anything a little harder than if you were getting wages

Cowboys lived and worked in an often hostile environment, and some living quarters, such as these on a Woods County, Oklahoma, ranch, hardly suggested any of the comforts of home. Of notched-log construction with a sod roof, the structure offered sturdiness, if little else.

A cabin with outbuildings, corrals, and breaking pens on a Great Plains horse ranch.

Andrew Drumm's ranch in the Cherokee Outlet. Unlike many cattlemen during the beef bonanza, Drumm lived on his ranch in order to supervise the labor of his cowboys. He provided them with superior accommodations but underfed them in the belief that they would thus work harder. Drumm habitually awakened his men several hours before dawn, and some of them were known to ride out a few miles from the ranch, stake their horses, and sleep until sunrise.

A group of Oklahoma cowboys relaxing beside a shingled log cabin. The man seated, center, plays a fretless banjo, while the youngster atop a box at the far right strikes a pose, hand on pistol butt. Note the quarter of meat hanging from the tree, left, and the weather vane on the fence post in the foreground.

Cowboys branding calves on an Oklahoma ranch in 1889. Sidearms and fancy clothes are conspicuous by their absence. Smoke rises from the iron on the left.

Cowboys demonstrating their branding technique for the camera. The
iron is cold.

The first herd of whiteface cattle in the Oklahoma Panhandle, photographed during the summer of 1884. The group of riders at left includes a woman mounted sidesaddle and two small boys.

Roping, branding, and riding herd were not the cowboy's only chores. Here, at a dipping trough, cowboys work to move frightened cattle through hot disinfectant and keep them from climbing out. To record this scene, the photographer occupied, however briefly, a precarious perch.

g Cattle

A. A. Forbes, Photo

Mealtime during a roundup on the Diamond Ranch in Greer County, Oklahoma. The wagon at the right is loaded with firewood.

Cowboys pose with the remuda on a Woodward County, Oklahoma, ranch. Visible in their camp, pitched near a creek bottom, are a chuckwagon, rolls of bedding, and firewood. A small group of men stands near the cooking fire.

The noon meal on a Woodward County roundup. Cooking was often done in Dutch ovens, which were placed in trenches and covered with embers. Thus the shovel in the foreground.

A rancher and his wife visiting a Woodward County cow camp. Note the interior of the chuck box.

Bar-CC cowboys with their chuck wagon and remuda, photographed in the Texas-Oklahoma panhandle area in the 1890's.

A cowboy relaxes atop his horse and rolls a cigarette.

—and at the same time acquire all the knowledge and information possible, on the art of running cattle. Finally one of the Cow Boys on the ranch will quit, or get killed, and you being on hand, will get his place. Or some of the neighboring ranchmen might run short of hands, and knowing of you being out of employment will send after you.

Your wages will be all the way from $15.00 up to $40.00 per month, according to latitude. The further north or northwest you are the higher your wages will be—although on the northern ranges your expenses are more than they would be further south, on account of requiring warmer clothing and bedding during the long and severe winters.

After you have mastered the cow business thoroughly—that is, learned how not to dread getting into mud up to your ears, jumping your horse into a swollen stream when the water is freezing, nor running your horse at full speed, trying to stop a stampeded herd, on a dark night, when your course has to be guided by the sound of the frightened steer's hoofs—you command *good* wages, which will be from $25.00 to $60.00 per month, according to latitude as I said before.

If you are economical, you can save money very fast on the range, for your expenses, after your outfit is purchased, are very light—in fact almost nothing, if you don't use tobacco, gamble nor drink whiskey, when you strike a town.

There are some cattlemen who will let you invest your wages in cattle and keep them with theirs, at so much a head—about the average cost per head, per annum, of running the whole herd, which is a small fraction over $1.00.

Joseph Nimmo, Jr.

"A creature of circumstance"

1886

In 1885, Joseph Nimmo, Jr., chief of the United States Bureau of Statistics, produced a report of lasting value to historians of the western range-cattle industry. But the "Nimmo Report" (which was published under several titles in several different government documents) had little to say about the cowboy, concentrating instead on quantifiable data. The statistician spoke up, however, in *Harper's New Monthly Magazine* in November, 1886. Nimmo praised the cowboy and described him as performing an "important public service."

During the last fifteen years the American cow-boy has occupied a place sufficiently important to entitle him to a considerable share of public attention. His occupation is unique. In the exercise of his function he is always a man on horseback. His duty as a worker in the cattle business is at times to ride over the range in order to see that straying cattle do not rove too far from the assigned limits of the herd of which he has charge; at times to drive the herd from one locality to another; and at times to "round up" the dispersed cattle, by which is meant to collect them together for the purpose of branding calves, or of selecting beef cattle, which latter are driven to railroad stations for shipment to market. The chief qualifications of efficiency in this calling are courage, physical alertness, ability to endure exposure and fatigue, horsemanship, and skill in the use of the lariat.

From Joseph Nimmo, Jr., "The American Cow-Boy," *Harper's New Monthly Magazine*, Vol. LVII (November, 1886), 880–84.

The original cow-boy of this country was essentially a creature of circumstance, and mainly a product of western and southwestern Texas. Armed to the teeth, booted and spurred, long-haired, and covered with the broad-brimmed sombrero—the distinctive badge of his calling—his personal appearance proclaimed the sort of man he was.

The Texas cow-boys were frontiersmen, accustomed from their earliest childhood to the alarms and the struggles incident to forays of Indians of the most ferocious and warlike nature. The section of the State in which they lived was also for many years exposed to incursions of bandits from Mexico, who came with predatory intent upon the herds and the homes of the people of Texas. The carrying of fire-arms and other deadly weapons was consequently a prevalent custom among them. And being scattered over vast areas, and beyond the efficient protection and restraints of civil law, they of necessity became a law unto themselves.

It is not a strange thing that such an occupation and such environment should have developed a class of men whom persons accustomed to the usages of cultivated society would characterize as ruffians of the most pronounced type. But among the better disposed of the Texas cow-boys, who constitute, it is believed, much more than a majority of them, there were true and trusty men, in whom the dangers and fortunes of their lives developed generous and heroic traits of character. The same experiences, however, led the viciously inclined to give free vent to the worst passions. Upon slight provocation they would shoot down a fellow-man with almost as little compunction as they fired upon the wild beasts.

But the peculiar characteristics of the Texas cow-boys qualified them for an important public service. By virtue of their courage and recklessness of danger, their excellent horsemanship, and skill in the use of fire-arms, and by virtue also of the influence which they have exerted upon their gentler brethren of the northern ranges, they have been an efficient instrumentality in preventing Indian outbreaks, and in protecting the frontier settlements of the entire range and ranch cattle area against predatory incursions and massacres by Indians. This has been a natural result of the fact that the cow-boys constitute throughout that region a corps of mounted scouts, armed and equipped, twenty thousand strong. They traverse vast ranges, ford rivers, and search for cattle amid mountain fastnesses and in lurking-places of the river bottoms. No hostile movement could for a day escape their notice. It is certain that they have done much toward subduing a vast area to the arts of peace, and that an unarmed man may now travel alone throughout Wyoming, Dakota, Montana, and Idaho, and even in Texas, as safely as in the New England or the Middle States. As a pioneer of civilization the American cow-boy has therefore performed a public service which as fully entitles him to recognition as do the commercial results of his labors.

It is only twenty years since the discovery was made that between the line of settlement in Dakota, Nebraska, and Kansas at the east, and the Sierra Nevada and Coast ranges at the west, there was an area as large as the portion of the United States which is situated east of the Mississippi River, throughout which cattle could be raised and fattened on the open range, seeking their own food, water, and shelter without any aid from man, from the time they were dropped until they were in condition to be driven to a railroad station for shipment to market. This discovery, greater in its importance than the discovery of gold in California, or silver in Nevada, or petroleum in Pennsylvania, happened, according to the most reliable accounts, in this wise. Early in December, 1864, a government trader, with a wagon train of supplies drawn by oxen, was on his way west to Camp Douglas, in the Territory of Utah, but being overtaken on the Laramie Plains by an unusually severe snow-storm, he was compelled at once to go into winter-quarters. He turned his cattle adrift, expecting, as a matter of course, they would soon perish from exposure and starvation, but they remained about the camp, and as the snow was blown off the highlands the dried grass afforded them an abundance of forage. When the spring opened they were found to be in even better condition than when turned out to die four months previously. This at once led to the experiment of herding cattle on the northern ranges. But it was for years a slow and hazardous business. At that time it was the custom to allow the Indians upon the reservations to wander off during the summer months throughout the present range and ranch cattle area, in order that they might hunt buffaloes and other large game, and thus sustain themselves in their accustomed way until the approach of

winter, when they returned to their reservations to be again provided for by the government. Permission to depart on these expedi-
tions was always given upon the promise made to the military and
civil officers of the United States that while absent they would be
"good Indians." But as cattle were more easily caught than buffaloes,
they found it greatly to their advantage to swoop down upon the
herds, stampede them, and slaughter at their leisure as many as
their needs required. Oftentimes, by way of amusement, they
lifted the scalp of a stray cow-boy. In many instances they massacred
whole camps of settlers, whose chief occupation was cattle herding.
Occasionally these "wards of the nation" so far forgot themselves
as to put on war-paint and set the United States at defiance. The
massacre of General Custer and his detachment, on the 25th of
June, 1876, at Little Big Horn, Dakota, near the present location of
Fort Custer, led, however, to the adoption of a more stringent policy
on the part of the United States government with respect to requiring the Indians to remain upon their reservations. During the five
years following that tragic event our valiant little army, widely
scattered over a vast area, had many bloody encounters with the
savages. At last the spirit of resistance was broken, and Montana,
Idaho, and Dakota became comparatively safe for the introduction
of the range cattle business, which had already become known in
Colorado and Wyoming as a highly attractive enterprise and a
speedy avenue to wealth. As the work of the army drew nigh to
completion the cow-boy galloped in, and became the mounted
policeman of a vast area, always on patrol.

But even after the red man had retired to his reservation the lot
of the cattlemen was not entirely serene. From time immemorial the
horse-thief and the cattle-thief seem to have been a sort of parasitic
growth upon frontier life, apparently begotten of its conditions. So
it was on the range. For several years the entire region from Kansas
and Colorado at the south to Montana and Dakota at the north was
infested by cattle-thieves. The country afforded apparently illimit-
able scope for this nefarious traffic. It seemed at one time somewhat
a matter of doubt as to which should prosper most, the herdsmen or
the cattle-thieves. As the cattle of many proprietors intermingled
freely on vast ranges, it was comparatively easy and safe for a few
marauders to pounce down upon detached groups of cattle here and

there separated from the main body of the herds, and drive them off over some mountain range to a distant valley or range where grazing was abundant, and there brand the calves with a chosen hieroglyphic representative of a separate ownership, and change the marks of cattle already branded, by one or more dashes with a red-hot iron. It was clearly seen that in order to stamp out this new and threatening evil recourse must be had to a drastic remedy. Accordingly the various cattle associations organized a detective service, composed mainly of brave and trusty cow-boys, who were charged with the duty of reconnoitring the whole country in order to discover the miscreants in their lairs, also to watch for altered and surreptitious brands at the railroad shipping stations. In this way a large number of stolen cattle was recovered, and many cattle-thieves were apprehended. When the latter were arrested within the limits of the efficient administration of the law, they were handed over to the civil authorities. But when caught beyond the limits of organized counties, administrative justice was extemporized. The cattle-men and the cow-boys themselves supplied judges, jurymen, witnesses, attorneys, constables, and executioners. Sometimes a level-headed cow-boy was placed upon the judicial bench. The cattle-men assert that the extreme and only penalty was never inflicted except upon the clearest evidence of guilt.

When the verdict of guilty was pronounced, a short shrift, and a stout rope, and a grave without a coffin or a winding-sheet, ended the proceedings.

But a great change has taken place. On the northern ranges cattle stealing has become almost entirely a thing of the past. States and Territories have enacted laws requiring that all cattle shall be branded, and that the brands shall be recorded in the office of the clerk of the county in which the owner of each herd resides. The brands are also published. Thus the light of publicity is thrown upon the whole range cattle business, and at the same time it has acquired all those securities which characterize organized and well-ordered commercial enterprises.

At first the raising of cattle on the northern ranges was confined mainly to settlers possessed of small means. But soon men of enterprise and capital saw that the placing of great herds on the ranges of the north, as had been done for years in Texas and in Mexico, would, under adequate protection, be attended with great profit, for already railroads traversing or extending out into the Territories afforded the facilities for transporting cattle to the three great primary cattle markets of the United States, viz., Chicago, St. Louis, and Kansas City—Chicago being by far the largest—and thence to the markets of the world.

It was an enterprise which required both capital and courage. The State of Texas had for years been a prolific breeding ground for cattle. At that time cattle were worth on the ranges of that State but little more than their hides and tallow. Two-year-old steers could be purchased in almost unlimited numbers for from $3 50 to $4 50 a head. Besides, Texas had an army of cow-boys, who were acquainted with the Indian in all his ways, and who rather courted than refused a passage at arms with the savage. Here were therefore three material elements of success in a great undertaking—capital, cattle, and cow-boys. Intelligent enterprise came in and formed the combination, and not long afterward it became a matter of personal interest with the Indian to remain on his reservation all the year round. Speedily the Texas steer superseded the buffalo, and the cow-boy became the dominant power throughout New Mexico, Colorado, Wyoming, Montana, and the western portions of Dakota, Nebraska, and Kansas. Within the brief period of fifteen years the cordon of cattle interests was drawn so close around the Indian reservations that the monarch of the plains became "ye gentle savage."

As a general rule the ranch cattle business has, under good management, been wonderfully successful. Hundreds of men who a few years ago went into the business with exceedingly limited means have become "cattle kings," and now count their assets by hundreds of thousands and even by millions. In certain instances also women have embarked in the enterprise, and among the number are those who now rejoice in the sobriquet of "cattle queens."

The market value of the surplus product of the entire range and ranch cattle area during the year 1884 was about $40,000,000, aside from the consumption within that area. Besides, the increased value of herds during the year is estimated at quite as much more. Throughout that area the cattle business is the chief commercial enterprise; but as trade makes trade, it has been instrumental in creating important collateral and related trade interests. One of the most important results of this has been that the several transcontinental railroads have built up a large and profitable local traffic. The original conception of transcontinental traffic was that it would be confined almost entirely to "through business," but the local tonnage of the Northern Pacific Railroad during the year 1884 constituted ninety-five per cent of its total tonnage, and the local tonnage of the Union Pacific Railroad constituted forty-three per cent of its total tonnage.

The cow-boy of to-day, especially on the northern ranges, is of entirely different type from the original cow-boy of Texas. New conditions have produced the change. The range cattle business of Kansas, Nebraska, Colorado, Wyoming, Montana, and Dakota is, as already stated, a new business. Those engaged in it as proprietors are chiefly from the States situated east of the Missouri River and north of the Indian Territory. Among them are also many Englishmen, Scotchmen, Frenchmen, and Germans of large means, embracing titled men who have embarked in the business quite extensively. Many of these came to America originally as tourists or for the purpose of hunting buffaloes, but the attractiveness of the cattle business arrested them, and they have become virtually, if not through the act of naturalization, American herdsmen. Some of this class have, from the force of romantic temperament and the exhilaration of range life, themselves participated actively in the duties of the cow-boy.

Organization, discipline, and order characterize the new undertakings on the northern ranges. In a word, the cattle business of that section is now and has from the beginning been carried on upon strictly business principles. Under such proprietorships, and guided by such methods, a new class of cow-boys has been introduced and developed. Some have come from Texas, and have brought with them a knowledge of the arts of their calling, but the number from the other States and the Territories constitutes a large majority of the whole. Some are graduates of American colleges, and others of collegiate institutions in Europe. Many have resorted to the occupation of cow-boy temporarily and for the purpose of learning the range cattle business, with the view of eventually engaging in it on their own account, or in the interest of friends desirous of investing money in the enterprise.

The life of the cow-boy is always one of excitement and of romantic interest. His waking hours when "riding on trail" are spent in the saddle, and at night he makes his bed upon the lap of mother earth.

The great herds which are yearly driven out of Texas to the northern ranges usually embrace from 2500 to 4000 young cattle each, and the movement has since its beginning, about eighteen years ago, amounted to about 4,000,000 head, worth nearly $50,000,000. Each herd is placed in charge of a boss, with from eight to ten cow-boys, a provision wagon, and a cook. Four horses are supplied to each cow-boy, for the duty is an arduous one. The range cattle when away from their accustomed haunts are suspicious and excitable, and need to be managed with the greatest care to keep them from stampeding. When "on trail" they are "close herded" at nightfall, and all lie down within a space of about two acres. The cow-boys then by watches ride around them all night long. The sensible presence of man appears to give the animals a feeling of security.

The journey from southern Texas to Montana requires from four to six months. Herds are also driven from Oregon and Washington Territory to Wyoming and eastern Montana. It is impossible for one who has not had actual experience in "riding on trail" to imagine the difficulties involved in driving a large herd of wild cattle over mountain ranges, across desert lands where in some cases food and water are not found for many miles, and where streams must be crossed which are liable to dangerous freshets.

A large part of the northern ranges is embraced in the area which Silas Bent, an accomplished meteorologist, terms "the birthplace of the tornado." Thunder and lightning are here frequent, and they are especially terrifying to range cattle. The most thrilling incident in the life of the cow-boy occurs on the occasion of a thunderstorm at night. Such an occurrence is thus described from personal observation by Mr. William A. Baillie Grohman, an English writer:

"On the approach of one of these violent outbursts the whole force is ordered on duty; the spare horses—of which each man has always three, and often as many as eight or ten—are carefully fed and tethered, and the herd is 'rounded up,' that is, collected into as small a space as possible, while the men continue to ride around the densely massed herd. Like horses, cattle derive courage from the close proximity of man. The thunder peals, and the vivid lightning flashes with amazing brilliancy, as with lowered heads the herd eagerly watch the slow, steady pace of the cow-ponies, and no doubt derive from it a comforting sense of protection. Sometimes, however, a wild steer will be unable to control his terror, and will make a dash through a convenient opening. The crisis is at hand, for the example will surely be followed, and in two minutes the whole herd of 4000 head will have broken through the line of horsemen and be away, one surging, bellowing mass of terrified beasts. Fancy a pitch-dark night, a pouring torrent of rain, the ground not only entirely strange to the men, but very broken, and full of dangerously steep water-courses and hollows, and you will have a picture of cow-boy duty on such a night. They must head off the leaders. Once fairly off, they will stampede twenty, thirty, and even forty miles at a stretch, and many branches will stray from the main herd. Not alone the reckless rider, rushing headlong at breakneck pace over dangerous ground in dense darkness, but also the horses, small, insignificant beasts, but matchless for hardy endurance and willingness, are perfectly aware how much depends upon their speed that night, if it kills them. Unused till the last moment remains the heavy cowhide 'yuirt,' or whip, and the powerful spurs with rowels the size of five-shilling pieces. Urged on by a shout, the horses speed alongside the terrified steers until they manage to reach the leaders, when, swinging around, and fearless of horns, they press back the bellowing brutes till they turn them. All the men pursuing this manœuvre, the headlong rush is at last checked, and the leaders, panting and lashing their sides with their tails, are brought to a stand, and the whole herd is again 'rounded up.'"

Throughout the northern ranges sobriety, self-restraint, decent behavior, and faithfulness to duty are enjoined upon the cow-boys. A great improvement is also observable in the cow-boys of Texas. Deeds of violence among them are now few. The *morale* of the entire range and ranch cattle business of the United States now compares favorably with that of other large enterprises.

Charles Moreau Harger

"A man of unflinching courage"

1892

Charles Moreau Harger's "Cattle-Trails of the Prairies," which appeared in *Scribner's Magazine* in June, 1892, represents a journalist's attempt to write a popular capsule history of the range-cattle industry. Harger described the cowboy realistically and proved to be more adept at history than at prognostication. The cowboy, he concluded, was "a thing of the past."

The task of the drover and his assistant cow-boys in getting the herds from the Southern ranches to the Northern shipping points was one involving both skill and daring. Only a man of unflinching courage and quick movement could succeed in handling animals whose characteristics were rather those of the wild beast than of the creature bred for the sustenance of man. The Texas steer is no respecter of persons. For the man on horseback he has a wholesome fear; he seems to have something of the savage's conceit that the combination is irresistible. Separately, neither man nor horse has any more chance in a herd fresh from the range than among so many wolves or jackals. With their long, sharp-pointed horns these steers rend an enemy with ease, and the fights among themselves have all the ferociousness of contests in the jungle.

The first contact between the cow-boys and the cattle is at the annual round-up, when the whole territory over which the owner's

From Charles Moreau Harger, "Cattle-Trails of the Prairies," *Scribner's Magazine*, Vol. XI (June, 1892), 732–42.

herds range is gone over and the cattle gathered for branding. The offspring are given the mark of the mother, and the ranch-owner possesses a brand as exclusively as does a manufacturer a trade-mark. After the young have been lassoed, held, and had their flesh burned with the red-hot branding-iron, leaving a scar in the form of a letter, figure, or combination design that will last for life, they are turned loose and no human hand is laid on them until they become "beeves," that is, four years old and ready for market. The cow-boys live in cabins near the water-courses and watch the stock from day to day, sometimes having the herds ten or twenty miles away. Should any "mavericks," that is, unbranded stock over one year old, get with the herd, they become the property of the person branding them, hence no inconsiderable addition is frequently made to a herd by this means....

Spring was the usual starting time, and during the seasons of the large drives, May, June, July, and August saw almost a solid procession passing over the great trails. So near were the herds that the drivers could hear one another urging along the stock, and frequently even the utmost care could not prevent two companies stampeding together, entailing a loss of much time and labor in separating them.

Once started, it was remarkable the orderly manner in which a herd took its way across the plains. A herd of a thousand beeves would string out to a length of two miles, and a larger one still longer. It made a picturesque sight. The leaders were flanked by cow-boys on wiry Texas ponies, riding at ease in great saddles with high backs and pommels. At regular distances were other riders, and the progress of the cavalcade was not unlike that of an army on a march. There was an army-like regularity about the cattle's movements, too. The leaders seemed always to be especially fitted for the place, and the same ones would be found in the front rank throughout the trip; while others retained their relative positions in the herd day after day.

At the start there was hard driving, twenty to thirty miles a day, until the animals were thoroughly wearied. After that twelve to fifteen miles was considered a good day's drive, thus extending the journey over forty to one hundred days. The daily programme was as regular as that of a regiment on the march. From morning until

noon the cattle were allowed to graze in the direction of their desti-
nation, watched by the cow-boys in relays. The cattle by this time
were uneasy and were turned into the trail and walked steadily
forward eight or ten miles, when, at early twilight, they were halted
for another graze. As darkness came on they were gathered closer
and closer into a compact mass by the cow-boys riding steadily in
constantly lessening circles around them, until at last the brutes lay
down, chewing their cuds and resting from the day's trip. Near
midnight they would usually get up, stand awhile, and then lie down
again, having changed sides. At this time extra care was necessary to
keep them from aimlessly wandering off in the darkness. Sitting on
their ponies, or riding slowly round and round their reclining
charges, the cow-boys passed the night on sentinel duty, relieving
one another at stated hours.

When skies were clear and the air bracing, the task of cattle-
driving was a pleasant and healthful one. But there came rainy days,
when the cattle were restless, and when it was anything but enjoy-
able riding through the steady downpour. Then especially were the
nights wearisome, and the cattle were ready at any time to stampede.

No one could tell what caused a stampede, any more than one
can tell the reason of the strange panics that attack human gather-
ings at times. A flash of lightning, a crackling stick, a wolf's howl,
little things in themselves, but in a moment every horned head was
lifted, and the mass of hair and horns, with fierce, frightened eyes
gleaming like thousands of emeralds, was off. Recklessly, blindly, in
whatever direction fancy led them, they went, over a bluff or into
a morass, it mattered not, and fleet were the horses that could keep
abreast of the leaders. But some could do it, and lashing their ponies
to their best gait the cow-boys followed at breakneck speed. Getting
on one side of the leaders the effort was to turn them, a little at first,
then more and more, until the circumference of a great circle was
being described. The cattle behind blindly followed, and soon the
front and rear joined and "milling" commenced. Like a mighty mill-
stone, round and round the bewildered creatures raced until they
were wearied out or recovered from their fright.

To stop the herd from milling, either after a stampede or when
in the cattle-yards at the end of the trip, was a necessary but difficult task. As in a stampede, it was death to an animal who failed to

keep up with his comrades, for in a moment his carcass would be flattened by thousands of trampling hoofs. The human voice seemed the most powerful influence that could be used to affect the brutes, force being entirely out of the question. As soon as the "milling" began the cow-boys began to sing. It mattered not what so long as there was music to it, and it was not uncommon to hear some profane and heartless bully doling out camp-meeting hymns to soothe the ruffled spirits of a herd of Texas steers, a use which might have astonished the fathers and mothers of the churches "back in God's country," could they have known of it.

A stampede always meant a loss, and rendered the herd more likely to be again panic-stricken. Certain hysterical leaders were frequently shot because of their influence on the remainder of the column. Another danger was that of the mingling of two herds; while in the earlier days the presence of buffalo was a decided peril. A herd of buffalo roaring and tearing its way across the plain was almost certain to cause a panic, if within hearing, and outriders were necessary to watch for these enemies and turn their course from the trail. Besides, marauding Indians were always to be feared, and many a skirmish was had between the cow-boys and red-skins. An understanding with the chiefs was, however, usually sufficient to insure safety. Thus accompanied by incidents that brought into play all the strength and strategy of their guards, the horned host moved on. Rivers were crossed by swimming in the same order that had been followed on land.

Reaching the outskirts of the shipping-station the herd was held on the plains until the drover effected a sale or secured cars for shipment. Then the animals were driven into the stockades, dragged or coaxed into the cars, and were sent off to meet their fate in the great packing-houses. The journey had been a strange one to them, often accompanied by savage cruelties at the hands of heartless drivers, and the end of the trip with close confinement of yard and car, the first they had ever known, was strangest of all.

With the loading of the cattle came the "paying off" and the cow-boy's brief vacation before returning to another year's round of hard work and coarse fare. It was not, perhaps, to be expected that after nearly a twelvemonth of life on the prairies he should spend his

Two Oklahoma cowboys, John and Dal Dunn, pose for the camera in 1892.

A cowboy and his horse pose in the littered alley of a western town. Neither is attired for the occasion. Note the muddy stirrups.

Five Texas cowboys, with high-heeled boots and ropes.

Some of the best cowboys were Indians. A cattleman once told General James S. Brisbin that Indian herders were "the best in the world. The Pawnee Indian is a natural herder, and if I had a million head of cattle I would place them all under Pawnee herders." These cowboys, possibly Caddo or Kickapoo Indians, were photographed in Woodward County, Oklahoma. Several are wearing moccasins.

An Osage Indian cowboy photographed in his fancy clothes by C. I. Hak, of Chicago. The lettering on his belt buckle indicates that he attended Carlisle Indian School.

A portrait of a cowboy, with his arsenal and tooled saddle and bridle,
taken in a Caldwell, Kansas, studio.

Demonstrating something less than enthusiasm in this extreme version of cowboy garb is Dodge City's Fred E. Sutton, alias the "Crooked S Kid," in a studio portrait.

outing in quiet and dignity. And seldom indeed did he. The cattle towns catered to his worst passions, and saloons and dance-houses flourished with startling exuberance. Gambling ran riot, and quarrels ending in murder were of frequent occurrence. During the height of the season might was the only law, and if occasionally a marshal was found, like William Hickok, the original Wild Bill, who could rule an Abilene in its rudest period, it was because he was quicker with the revolver and more daring than even the cow-boys themselves.

Much glamour and romance have been thrown around the figure of the cow-boy. He was not the dashing and chivalric hero of the burlesque stage, in gorgeous sombrero and sash, nor was he the drunken, fighting terror of the dime novel. He was a very average Westerner, dressed for comfort, and with the traits of character that his business induced. The cow-boy lived a hard life. For months he never saw a bed, nor slept beneath a roof. He seldom had access to a newspaper or book, and had none of society's advantages to lift him to higher things. The roughest of the West's immigrants, as well as many Mexicans, drifted into the business because of its excitement and good wages, and this class by its excesses gave the world its standard for all. With the influences of actual contact with bucking bronco ponies and ferocious Texas steers, themselves by no means elevating, added to the temptations of the cattle towns, all the worst in the herder's nature was sure to be brought out. But hundreds of cow-boys were sons of Christian parents, and when they had made a start in life settled down at last as good citizens of the great West they had helped to develop.

The cow-boy with his white, wide-rimmed hat, his long leathern cattle whip, his lariat, and his clanking spur is a thing of the past. The great Texas ranches are enclosed with barbed wire fences, and a genuine Texas steer would attract almost as much attention in the old cattle towns as a llama. Abilene, Ellsworth, Newton, and Dodge City are busy little cities surrounded by rich farming communities and with churches, schools, electric lights, and other evidences of modern civilization. No trace of the old life remains, except some weather-stained and dilapidated buildings, pointed out to the stranger as having been saloons where Wild Tom, Texas Sam, or other strangely named characters, killed men unnumbered "during the cattle days." But even these traditions are known to but few of the modern inhabitants, so entirely has a new people filled the land in the last decade.

The cattle-trails were in a measure educative. They brought the north and south of the Mississippi Valley into close business relations, a condition which was to the advantage of both. But the life that surrounded them could not endure. The homes of thousands of settlers have pre-empted the grazing grounds. Railroads are ten times more numerous than were the trails, and like the cavalier, the troubadour, the Puritan, and the "Forty-niner," the cow-boy and his attendant life have become but figures in history.

Richard Harding Davis

"There are cowboys and cowboys"

1892

According to Fred Lewis Pattee, Richard Harding Davis was "the most widely known reporter of his generation." He became managing editor of *Harper's Weekly* in 1890, and in January, 1892, he began a tour of the West that resulted in a series of articles for *Harper's Monthly*. They were collected and published in book form under the title *The West from a Car-Window*. Davis visited briefly, wrote quickly, and dealt largely with surface appearances.

The coming of the barb-wire fence and the railroad killed the cowboy as a picturesque element of recklessness and lawlessness in south-west Texas. It suppressed him and localized him and limited him to his own range, and made his revolver merely an ornament. Before the barb-wire fence appeared, the cattle wandered from one range to another, and the man of fifteen thousand acres would overstock, knowing that when his cattle could not find enough pasturage on his range they would move over to the range of his more prosperous neighbor. Consequently, when the men who could afford it began to fence their ranges, the smaller owners who had over-bred, saw that their cattle would starve, and so cut the fences in order to get back to the pastures which they had used so long. This, and the shutting off of water-tanks and of long-used trails brought on the barb-wire fence wars which raged long and fiercely between the

From Richard Harding Davis, *The West from a Car-Window* (New York, Harper & Brothers, 1892), 135–48.

cowboys and fence men of rival ranches and the Texas Rangers. The barb-wire fences did more than this; they shut off the great trails that stretched from Corpus Christi through the Pan Handle of Texas, and on up through New Mexico and Colorado and through the Indian Territory to Dodge City. The coming of the railroad also made this trailing of cattle to the markets superfluous, and almost destroyed one of the most remarkable features of the West. This trail was not, of course, an actual trail, and marked as such, but a general driveway forty miles wide and thousands of miles long. The herds of cattle that were driven over it numbered from three hundred to three thousand head, and were moving constantly from the early spring to the late fall.

No caravan route in the far Eastern countries can equal this six months' journey through three different States, and through all changes of weather and climate, and in the face of constant danger and anxiety. This procession of countless cattle on their slow march to the north was one of the most interesting and distinctive features of the West.

An "outfit" for this expedition would consist of as many cowboys as were needed to hold the herd together, a wagon, with the cook and the tents, and extra ponies for the riders. In the morning the camp-wagon pushed on ahead to a suitable resting-place for the night, and when the herd arrived later, moving, on an average, fifteen miles a day, and grazing as it went, the men would find the supper ready and the tents pitched. And then those who were to watch that night would circle slowly around the great army of cattle, driving them in closer and closer together, and singing as they rode, to put them to sleep. This seems an absurdity to the Eastern mind, but the familiar sounds quieted and satisfied these great stupid animals that can be soothed like a child with a nursery rhyme, and when frightened cannot be stopped by a river. The boys rode slowly and patiently until one and then another of the herd would stumble clumsily to the ground, and others near would follow, and at last the whole great herd would be silent and immovable in sleep. But the watchfulness of the sentries could never relax. Some chance noise—the shaking of a saddle, some cry of a wild animal, or the scent of distant water carried by a chance breeze across the prairie, or nothing but sheer blind wantonness—would start one of the sleeping mass to his feet with a snort, and in an instant the whole great herd would go tearing madly over the prairie, tossing their horns and bellowing, and filled with a wild, unreasoning terror. And then the skill and daring of the cowboy was put to its severest test, as he saw his master's income disappearing towards a cañon or a river, or to lose itself in the brush. And the cowboy who tried to head off and drive back this galloping army of frantic animals had to ride a race that meant his life if his horse made a misstep; and as the horse's feet often did slip, there would be found in the morning somewhere in the trail of the stampeding cattle a horrid mass of blood and flesh and leather.

Do you wonder, then, after this half-year of weary, restless riding by day, and sleepless anxiety and watching under the stars by night, that when the lights of Dodge City showed across the prairie, the cowboy kicked his feet out of his stirrups, drove the blood out of the pony's sides, and "came in to town" with both guns going at once, and yelling as though the pent-up speech of the past six months of loneliness was striving for proper utterance?

The cowboy cannot be overestimated as a picturesque figure; all that has been written about him and all the illustrations that have been made of him fail to familiarize him, and to spoil the picture he makes when one sees him for the first time racing across a range outlined against the sky, with his handkerchief flying out behind, his sombrero bent back by the wind, and his gauntlets and broad leather leggings showing above and at the side of his galloping pony. And his deep seat in the saddle, with his legs hanging straight to the long stirrups, the movement of his body as it sways and bends, and his utter unconsciousness of the animal beneath him would make a German riding-master, an English jockey, or the best cross-country rider of a Long Island hunting club shake his head in envy and despair.

He is a fantastic-looking individual, and one suspects he wears the strange garments he affects because he knows they are most becoming. But there is a reason for each of the different parts of his apparel, in spite of rather than on account of their picturesqueness. The sombrero shades his face from the rain and sun, the rattlesnake-skin around it keeps it on his head, the broad kerchief that he wears knotted around his throat protects his neck from the heat, and the leather leggings which cover the front of his legs protect them from the cactus in Texas, and in the North, where the fur and hair are left on the leather, from the sleet and rain as he rides against them. The gauntlets certainly seem too military for such rough service, but any one who has had a sheet rope run through his hands, can imagine how a lasso cuts when a wild horse is pulling on the other end of it. His cartridge-belt and his revolver are on some ranches superfluous, but cattle-men say they have found that on those days when they took this toy away from their boys, they sulked and fretted and went about their work half-heartedly, so that they believe it pays better to humor them, and to allow them to relieve the monotony of the day's vigil by popping at jack-rabbits and learning to twirl their revolver around their first finger. Of the many compliments I have heard paid by officers and privates and ranch-owners and cowboys to Mr. Frederic Remington, the one which was sure to follow the others was that he never made the mistake of putting the revolver on the left side. But as I went North, his anonymous admirers would make this same comment, but with regret that he should be guilty of such an error. I could not understand this at first until I found that the two sides of the shield lay in the Northern cowboy's custom of wearing his pistol on the left, and of the Texan's of carrying it on the right. The Northern man argues on this important matter that the sword has always been worn on the left, that it is easier to reach across and sweep the pistol to either the left or right, and that with this motion it is at once in position. The Texan says this is absurd, and quotes the fact that the pistol-pocket has always been on the right, and that the lasso and reins are in the way of the left hand. It is too grave a question of etiquette for any one who has not at least six notches on his pistol-butt to decide.

Although Mr. Kleberg's cowboys have been shorn of their pistols, their prowess as ropers still remains with them. They gave us an exhibition of this feature of their calling which was as remarkable a performance in its way as I have ever seen. The audience seated itself on the top of a seven-rail fence, and thrilled with excitement. At least a part of it did. I fancy Mr. Kleberg was slightly bored, but he was too polite to show it. Sixty wild horses were sent into a pen eighty yards across, and surrounded by the seven-rail fence. Into this the cowboys came, mounted on their ponies, and at Mr. Kleberg's word lassoed whichever horse he designated. They threw their ropes as a man tosses a quoit, drawing it back at the instant it closed over the horse's head, and not, as the beginner does, allowing the noose to settle loosely, and to tighten through the horse's effort to move forward. This roping was not so impressive as what followed, as the ropes were short, owing to the thick undergrowth, which prevents long throws, such as are made in the North, and as the pony was trained to suit its gait to that of the animal it was pursuing, and to turn and dodge with it, and to stop with both forefeet planted firmly when the rope had settled around the other horse's neck.

But when they had shown us how very simple a matter this was, they were told to dismount and to rope the horses by whichever foot Mr. Kleberg chose to select. This was a real combat, and was as intensely interesting a contest between a thoroughly wild and terrified animal and a perfectly cool man as one can see, except, perhaps, at a bullfight. There is something in a contest of this sort that has appealed to something in all human beings who have blood in their veins from the days when one gladiator followed another with a casting-net and a trident around the arena down to the present, when "Peter" Poe drops on one knee and tries to throw Hefflefinger over his shoulder. In this the odds were in favor of the horse, as a cowboy on the ground is as much out of his element as a sailor on a horse, and looks as strangely. The boys moved and ran and backed away as quickly as their heavy leggings would permit; but the horses moved just twice as quickly, turning and jumping and rearing, and then racing away out of reach again at a gallop. But whenever they came within range of the ropes, they fell. The roping around the neck had seemed simple. The rope then was cast in a loop with a noose at one end as easily as one throws a trout line. But now the rope had to be hurled as quickly and as surely as a man sends a ball to first base when the batsman is running, except that the object at which the cowboy aims is moving at a gallop, and one of a galloping horse's four feet is a most uncertain bull's-eye.

It is almost impossible to describe the swiftness with which the rope moved. It seemed to skim across the ground as a skipping-rope does when a child holds one end of it and shakes the rope up and down to make it look like a snake coiling and undulating over the pavement.

One instant the rope would hang coiled from the thrower's right hand as he ran forward to meet the horse, moving it slowly, with a twist of his wrist, to keep it from snarling, and the next it would spin out along the ground, with the noose rolling like a hoop in the front, and would close with a snap over the horse's hoof, and the cowboy would throw himself back to take the shock, and the horse would come down on its side as though the ground had slipped from under it.

The roping around the neck was the easy tossing of a quoit; the roping around the leg was the angry snapping of a whip.

There are thousands of other ranches in the United States besides those in Texas, and other cowboys, but the general characteristics are the same in all, and it is only general characteristics that one can attempt to give.

W. S. James

"The cow-boy goes to the school of nature"

1898

W. S. James (not to be confused with cowboy author and illustrator Will James) was, says J. Frank Dobie, a "genuine cowboy." Cow-punching must have had a salutary effect on him, because he later became a preacher. His memoir, *Cow-Boy Life in Texas, or 27 Years a Mavrick*, was published in 1898. This selection provides an interesting contrast to Siringo's narrative.

In writing on the subject of "Life on a Texas Ranch," I don't wish it understood that there is any cast-iron rule by which one shall judge of the manners and customs of the cow-man, for custom changes on the range as it does in any other section. The methods of work and customs differ as widely in different localities as do the dress of women, and if this is not giving a sufficiently wide range I don't know how to express it. The ranches in southern Colorado and western New Mexico, as well as the "Panhandle of Texas," were conducted on widely different plans, to the ranches in middle and western Texas, and again in the southern part of the State there was a marked difference.

I am treating of the special features of ranch life as noticeable in central and western Texas, being the range with which I was most familiar. It is true I had some experience in various ranges and more observation than actual experience, but my substantial knowledge

From W. S. James, *Cow-Boy Life in Texas, or 27 Years a Mavrick* [*sic*] (Chicago, M. A. Donohue & Co., 1898), 79–100.

is confined to the locality above named. While the cattle-man is not a straight-edge, has no cast-iron rule as the guide of his life in handling cattle, still take him wherever you find him and he is much the same in many respects. Many people think the cow-boy is an ignoramus as far as books are concerned, and many of them have had but meagre advantages, but many more have been educated in some of the best institutions in the country.

Out of nine young men, the oldest one in the squad being twenty-eight, who were lounging around a campfire one evening, or night as it is termed in the South, after supper, singing, telling stories and having such a jolly time as can only be enjoyed round a camp-fire when every one is duly sober, the conversation turned upon education, and it was ascertained by taking stock that five out of the nine had graduated in Eastern colleges, two of the five being U. V. graduates, and every one of the remaining four having enjoyed the advantages of a common school education.

Yet his education is not especially in letters, except as they are used for brands on cattle. Neither is it simply from A to Z, in lines. It is all round, up and down, over, under and between. Wherever you strike him he is at home, he knows his lesson. They are unlike some people to be met with in life who pass current as scholars, but when taken out of their books, don't know straight up.

The cow-boy goes to the school of nature, learns his lesson from observation and practical experience. He goes by no stipulated rules, cuts no square corners, but takes his bearing and goes straight on. This is the general rule, to which there are exceptions. The manners and practices of different men in camp are as varied as anywhere on earth, some men are good at one thing and no good at another, some are careless of their personal appearance, while others are very careful, but if they fall into lines anywhere it is in point of dress; even the cook will fall into wearing good clothes, especially a good hat, good boots, good pants and overshirt. One man we had in our outfit for years was fit for nothing under the sun but to break our saddle horses. I mean to ride them the first few days until they were sufficiently gentle to be ridden by less adventurous hands, but after a horse was once manageable he was utterly out of place on him. We kept him because he was the best rider that ever took work on the ranch. But the fellow, after a horse was bridle wise, would absolutely go to sleep riding along and sometimes a half tame-horse would suddenly take fright and began bucking, but he always kept his seat. I never, for the thirteen years I was associated with him, knew him to be thrown from a horse.

When we had no horses to handle if we worked him at all, it was on herd, and then it took one good hand and a boy part of the time to keep him awake (this of course is metaphorically speaking). Some men were good in holding a herd while cutting, some were good in cutting, some good in branding and the majority who stayed with the business were good all-round men. I mean by that, good most anywhere you put them, except the cook. He was the cook.

Some few good hands when on a round-up, and in general work, were no good in camp. Sometimes there would be no special cook and each would, or was supposed to, do his part, but they did not always do it. Some men would ride a tired horse into camp, take off the saddle, throw it on the ground just as it came handiest, maybe horn down; throw the wet blankets down on top of it all in a bunch; hopple him, pull the bridle off, and slash the poor fellow across the back with the bridle rein, thus forcing him to jump his poor tired bones out of range. Usually a man of this type would drop down in the shade of the grub wagon, or some tree and begin to order the cook round.

My observation has been that the man of this character never in the long run made a success in the cattle business. If he did, it was the exception, and was attributable to "nigger luck."

Another character would ride up, remove his saddle, hang it up or spread the skirts, spread his blankets, and lead his panting pony to grass, hopple him, smoothe his mane, speak kindly to him, remove the bridle, and come whistling or singing into camp; lay his bridle down, and look round to see if the water was out or anything short, he would roll up his sleeves, and, speaking kindly to the cook, fly in and help the fellow out.

The busiest time on a ranch is the preparations for the spring round-ups. There are saddles to mend, hopples to make, grub wagons to overhaul and horses to get in shape, shoeing and trimming up, quirts to make, ropes to straighten up, and planning till you can't rest. As there has been so much said and written about a round-up, and so many exaggerated stories told of riding broncho ponies,

I shall leave that for others to relate. Suffice it to say, out of every-thing that has been or can be written one can have a very inaccurate idea of the reality until he has been there and has witnessed it for himself.

But if you can draw on your imagination for a picture I will try to give you what you could see if you was to drive up to a ranch and find them making preparations for a round-up. I give it as I saw it last. Driving in from the north over a prairie country, with now and then a grove of trees, we picked our way down a winding hollow or ravine for one and a half miles, sometimes on one side of the hollow and then on the other. Finally we came out in the open valley that stretches for a mile or more down the creek on either side. Just on the opposite bank of the little creek stood the ranch house, the branding pens off to the west.

In front of the house stood the old grub wagon that had done service for years, with the barrel securely fastened to one side, the grub box sitting in the hind-most end of the bed, with its shelves, and door that dropped down. The cook is now busy cleaning it out—Johnny—God bless him! In fancy I see him now, as he stood there with sleeves rolled up, his pants turned up at the bottom. He had been working so hard the sweat was rolling off his dear old face. He was one of the best-hearted fellows I ever knew, one in whom the milk of human kindness was the predominant trait of character, and whose many virtues made him a universal favorite. He has long since gone to other pastures green.

Just beyond, and in front of the wagon, stood one of the boys, platting a whip. Astride the tongue of the wagon was Charley, mending his saddle, singing, as was his habit when busy. Out at the end of the house one of the boys was scraping some rawhide for hopples, and down the valley, perhaps a hundred yards away, one of the boys came leisurely driving some ponies, some of which still had the hopples on, being too rollicky to allow them taken off. Out on the wood-pile two of the outfit were earnestly trying to make a horse trade, while the remainder of the boys were in the pen branding some horses before starting out.

Now, if you wish to know it better, just go down and see for yourself, which you will hardly do, as that has been sixteen years ago, and everything has so changed as to make just such a thing almost an impossibility.

It is rather singular how ranches are named.

It is true that many ranches bear the names of the owners, as the Kieth ranch, Stone ranch, Campbell and Martin ranch, etc.; but many more go exclusively by the name of the brand, as the Cross-ell ranch (X L,) the Be-four ranch (B-4), the Diamond ranch (<>), the Block-er ranch (□ R,) Flower de Luce ranch, the Boot ranch (a boot), the Saddler ranch (a saddle and R).

The naming of horses was as a rule accidental. A new horse let fly and kicked at one of the boys, he went by the name of Heels until he passed in his chips. Another horse we had that was mean to kick never had any name but Dirty Heels. A little colt of fine blood that was left motherless and had to be raised on a bottle happened to come under the special care of one of the children, who one day remarked that it would be a wonder if he lived. He was called Wonder.

The same horse was afterward sold for $300, but still he remained a Wonder.

If an outfit bought a horse from a granger the horse almost invariably bore the name of his former owner, no difference how ugly it was. For illustration, we had one horse we got of a man by the name of Kizer, and Kizer was his name; one of a Mr. Dickey, and Dickey was his name. We had one that would put his teeth to a rail, tree or stump and draw as though he was sucking. We called him The Sucker. I might take your precious time for a week, and then not finish.

In naming creeks a chance circumstance would forever settle it. Father had a tussle with a wounded deer—a very large buck—one morning, the deer gave a peculiar whistle or snort, so common to them. The little hollow was, and is until this day, called Buck Snort.

The boys had been out for some weeks and run out of bread, the man they sent for it was delayed on account of rain and swollen streams, having to go sixty miles. We were camped on a little spring branch and had been living on beef straight for several days, when, our man came driving in with plenty of grub, the little hollow was ever afterward called Happy Hollow.

I knew a pony called Happy Jack, because of his contented disposition and his propensity to run and romp. Men were often nicknamed in the same way, but oftener from some peculiarity in their personal appearance. One man who measured six and one-half feet and weighed but 135 pounds was called Shorty; one on the contrary, only five feet four inches, was called Legs; a fellow who was extremely bow-legged was called Shanks. The cook as a rule was called Sallie.

One fellow, who sometimes tried to preach, and who, by the way, was recognized and respected by all the boys as a good man, while on a round-up allowed himself to become so excited one day, as to secure the sobriquet of Yaller. It came about in this way. We were traveling across a mountainous district and some of the boys off to the left side of the herd started a very large bear. Several of them joined in the chase, among them the preacher, who was riding an old yellow horse. As he was passing one of the boys, he was heard to say: "Git up and git, yaller, God bless you, git up and git." Some of the boys were sacrilegious enough to change it from Sunday-school language to something not so nice, but we didn't credit it. However, he was ever after called "Old Yaller." He killed the bear just the same.

I call no names in these short sketches, as many of the dear old boys are still living, and I would not wish to make public any property that is or has so long been "our own" private stock in trade.

Many of the men of whom I speak have gone from this to a better world. When the eternal spring shall come with its never withering grass, when the great Herald shall announce the final great round-up, it is to be hoped that the dear old boys will not all be turned in at the left-hand gate as strays to be "gobbled" up by the thief of human souls, but that they may be found to bear the Master's brand, and earmark of the redeemed of the Lord. . . .

If there is any one thing that has engaged the mind of the majority of the human family more than another in the past, it is the question of their personal appearance, and style or fashion has been as changeable as Texas weather, and I dare say the locality and peculiar people that never change style are the exception. If one should wish to know anything about the rural districts of Old Mexico, they would have to go back four or five thousand years and read in Genesis, but only give them time and they too will change.

In the mountains of eastern Tennessee and the swamps of Louisiana and Arkansas, as well as the piney woods of eastern Texas, they have changed from the old flint-lock to the cap and ball gun, and some of them have quit making their own clothing and wear store clothes, because it is stylish now to wear brown duck instead of "jeans." The cow-boy is no exception to the rule. He has his flights of fancy as clearly defined as the most fashionable French belle.

In 1867, I remember distinctly the style that prevailed, flowing toefenders, narrow stirrup, and the rider stood on his toe. The saddle at that time was almost anything that could be had, but preferably the broad horn standing at an angle of forty-five degrees, pointing heavenward. The bridle was hardly to be called a creation of fancy, as it was all they had, and was made from the hide of a cow, rubbed and grained until it was pliable.

Some men broke the monotony by adopting the Mexican plan of making them of hair, which was a very popular article of which to make ropes. Some made their bridles of rawhide by platting, which made quite an artistic one, some would plait the quirt on the end of the rein. The rope used for catching and handling horses and cattle was a platted one and was one of the best ropes for the purpose I ever used. I have seen a few ropes that were very good, made of rawhide, of three strands twisted and run together. In fact, during, and for several years after the war, long after reconstruction days in Texas, it was said—and not without some foundation—that a Texan could take a butcher knife and rawhide and make a steamboat, of course he could not have made the boiler, but when it came to the top part he would have been at home. One thing certain, if the thing had broken to pieces, he could have tied it up.

During the war his clothing was made from home-spun cloth, he had no other, home-made shoes or boots, even his hat was home-made, the favorite hat material being straw. Rye straw was the best. Sometimes a fellow would get hold of a Mexican hat, and then he was sailing.

The popular way for protecting the clothing, was to make a leather cap for the knee and seat of the pants, the more enterprising would make leggins of calf-skin, hair out, and sometimes buckskin with fringe down the side.

By 1872 most everything on the ranch had undergone a change, even some of the boys had changed their range headquarters for sunnier climes, because they had to, some had sold out to a lawyer and had taken a contract from the State; others had changed their spurs and leggins for a crown, harp and wings, and gone to pastures green, perhaps. But especially had style changed, the wool hat, the leather leggins, leather bridle and the broad stirrup; the invention of an old fellow who lived on the Llano river had become so popular that one who was not provided with them was not in the style.

The stirrup was from six to eight inches broad, and the rider drew his leathers so as to ride with legs crooked up considerably. The saddle used was one with a broad flat horn, much higher in front than behind, adorned with saddle pockets, covered with either goat or bear skin. The spur too was another article that changed, the long shank with bells had taken the place of the little straight shank and sharp rowel, the long ones making a curve downward and having long teeth rowels. In this age of the cow-man they wore buckskin gloves with long gauntlets.

The style changed again by '77. The John B. Stetson hat with a deeper crown and not so broad a rim, and the ten-ounce hat took the cake. Up to this date, the high-heeled boots were the rage, and when it was possible to have them, the heel was made to start under the foot, for what reason I never knew, unless it was the same motive that prompts the girls to wear the opera heel in order to make a small track, thus leaving the impression that a number ten was only a six, this I am guessing at and will leave it open for the reader to draw to. By the last named date, '77 or '78, the cow-man had in many places adopted the box-toed boot with sensible heels, and the California saddle was taking the place of all others. This was an extremely heavy saddle, with a small horn but very strong and the most comfortable saddle to be found for steady use, and as a rule, the easiest one on a horse.

There was another saddle, a Texas production, closely allied to the Bucharia, but not so heavy, that was, and is to this day, a very popular saddle. The slicker and tarpaulin were two of the most valuable accessions to the cow-man's outfit that ever came into the business. They were made of good cotton stuff, and a preparation of linseed oil filled every pore so completely that they were as thoroughly waterproof as a shingle roof, and became the cow-boy's right bower.

A cow-boy's outfit is never complete except he has a good supply of hopples on hand. After sea-grass ropes became so plentiful and cheap, the good old rawhide hopples and platted lariettes were relegated to the rear, and if the cow-pony could talk, unless he was a good, religious pony, he would curse the day when sea-grass hopples were introduced. His feelings toward the inventor of that article would be something like those of the native toward the barbed-wire manufacturer, for the poor little fellows sometimes wore a very sore pair of legs by the use of the strand of a rope for a hopple.

There has been much said about pack-ponies, and that method of working a range, by taking the grub on a pack. Some very amusing things will occur with the pack. I remember once, while driving through Waco, the pack-pony became a little unruly, and was running up and down street after street, when the pack slipped and turned under. This put the little gentleman to kicking. The result was that flour, bacon, beans, tincups and plates, coffee-pot, sugar, onions and bedding were strewn over about five acres of ground. Some of the boys suggested that we hire the ground broke and harrowed before it rained and thus secure a good crop of grub.

The pack-pony was very handy, but the greatest trouble of any one thing in the outfit, and it was the most cruel thing imaginable to fasten the pack on so as to make it secure, even with a saddle, and fasten it well, let the pony or donkey, as the case might be, run into a pond of water and get the ropes wet; it was terrible on him. When an outfit had to resort to a pack, they usually hired their bread made, or made it sometimes, when they couldn't find a woman, not infrequently making it up in the mouth of the sack, and if they had no skillet would either fry it or cook it hoe-cake fashion; but I have seen it cooked by rolling the dough round a stick and holding it over the fire, turning it until cooked.

The change in the styles of saddles brought the change, also, in the stirrup. Since '78, and the introduction of the California saddle, the narrow stirrup has been used, and has been found to be the most comfortable. The change in position of the legs, too, accompanied this change in the fashion. The foot is thrust through the stirrup until the stirrup rests in the hollow of the foot, or the foot rests thus in the stirrup, just as you like, and when the rider sits in his saddle the straps are lengthened so as to let him rest his weight just comfortably in the stirrup, while at the same time he is not removed from the saddle-seat.

It has been fully demonstrated that the man who rides thus, and sits straight on his horse, is capable of riding farther, and with less fatigue to himself and horse, than one who is all the time changing.

The methods of handling cattle change as well as the paraphernalia. I remember it was a rare thing ever to see a man branding cattle on horseback. If they did, they usually threw the rope on the animal's head, and then tied them to a tree and heeled them, or threw the rope round their hind legs and simply stretched them out. In branding yearlings or calves on the range, they would make a run, toss the tug on the animal; one man would hold while another would dismount, catch it by the tail, jerk it down, draw its tail between its hind legs, place his knee against its back while it would be lying on its side, and thus hold it while the first man would brand and mark it. In the way described above, one man could hold the largest animal on the range, if he understood his business. Range-branding was a very popular method of branding mavericks. The necessary outfit usually was a sharp knife, a straight bar and half circle; the ring end of a wagon rod, or common iron rings, were good. In the case of using rings, one needed a pair of pincers. However, one used to such work, could very successfully run a brand with them by using a couple of sticks, with which to hold them.

For many years, however, the custom was to drive the cattle to some pen, many of which were located over each range, and then brand up all those that belonged to any one in the outfit, or those they knew, and sometimes a miracle would be performed by branding all those left in the brand of the cows they followed, and if any were left whose owner was not known, and was too old to claim a mother, they were—well, I can't exactly say, as I was not always by, but usually those whose mothers were strays were turned out and left to run until they were too old to be known. In after years they were usually dealt with differently.

The style changed to catching cattle as well as horses by the front feet or fore feet, as we called them, which was a much better method of throwing them.

The horse when roped by the head if wild, will choke himself down and the best method of holding him when once down is to take him by the ear with one hand, nose with the other. To illustrate, if the horse falls on his left side you want to take hold of his ear with your right hand and nose with the left hand, raising it until his mouth is at an angle of forty, five degrees, placing one knee on his neck near his head. In this way a small man can hold a large horse on the ground.

The difference in holding a horse and cow down is that you must hold the horse's front legs or head on the ground because he never gets up behind first but throws his front feet out and then gets up: the cow on the contrary gets up directly the reverse, gets up on her hind feet first, therefore you must hold her down by the tail. The horse is easily choked down but it is almost an impossibility to choke a cow down. It is a noted fact that a colt that is handled when sucking, being staked and becoming used to a rope between the time he is two months and a year old, is never very wild. He may be hard to drive when allowed to run with wild horses but when once in hand is easily managed. The cow on the other hand may be raised perfectly gentle and if allowed to run out and become wild, may become the most vicious of any other.

Speaking of the method of holding cattle and horses down calls to mind a little incident that came under my observation. A cattleman employed a Swede who was a very stout fellow, he was as willing as he was green, and was green enough to make up for all his other virtues. This cattleman was not over-sensitive about what another had to perform. One day they roped a wild horse of good size and when they had choked him until he fell to the ground, the cow-man called to the Swede "Jump on his head," meaning, of course, for him to catch the horse as before described but instead of that the ignorant fellow jumped right astride the horse's head and the rope being slacked the horse made a lunge and threw the poor fellow his length on the ground and ran over him. It seemed a miracle if he came out alive but he only received a few bruises.

At another time when handling a bad cow, the same parties

engaged, the cow made a run at the Swede when his boss called to him to catch her by the horns which he did and the cow simply lifted him a double somersault over her back. He eventually got tired and quit the cattle business, went to farming and, as a good story book would say, "did well and lived happy ever afterward."

Those who think the cow-boy is not stylish simply let them hunt him up, study his character, note his fancy and while it is true that like poor Yorick of old he is "a fellow of infinite jest, of most peculiar fancy," still he is stylish after a fashion of his own.

To say that any law of fashion does or could wield an influence over him, I think, would be a mistake. I don't think one could be induced to wear a plug hat. If he did at all it would be for the novelty of the thing. If you see him in New York or Chicago you see him wearing the same sort of a hat and boots he wears at home.

He is looked upon by some as a law breaker. It is true in some cases, but is it not equally true of all classes? I maintain that it is not more universal with this than any other class of men in any one vocation of life. It may be a little more out-breaking but of the same kind. His wild free range and constant association with nature and natural things makes him more sensitive to restraint than he otherwise would be. Under the influences of a free wild life he has grown to be self-reliant and like Davie Crocket, "he asks no favors and shuns no responsibilities;" he, however, measures his responsibilities by a rule of his own construction which is oftener the outgrowth of personal inclination than a well balanced consciousness of moral responsibility, like his brother of more favorable surroundings who is prone to reject the moral teachings of God's word and fall back for a refuge to the unreliable guidance of conscience; when this moral guide has been so educated as to be like the material of which he makes his hopples which, by a little dampening and working becomes pliable, has a tendency to stretch and thus meet the demands of its environments.

The cow-boy's outfit of clothing, as a rule, is of the very best from hat to boots, he may not have a dollar in the world, but he will wear good, substantial clothing, even if he has to buy it on a credit, and he usually has plenty of that, that is good. I once heard a minister in a little Northern town, in using the cow-boy as an illustration, say "The cow-boy with an eighteen dollar hat and a two dollar suit of clothing is as happy as a king on his throne," or words to that effect.

With those who knew no better the illustration perhaps held good, but to a crowd of the boys it would have been very ridiculous and amusing. In fact extravagance is one of the cow-boy's failings. The inventory of his wardrobe could be very correctly summed up as follows: Hat, five to ten dollars; pants, five to ten dollars; coat and vest, from eight to twenty dollars; overshirt, from three to five dollars, and everything else to match. They may be cheated in buying, but are never beat by the same man the second time, they at least think they are getting the best, and always make the best of their bargain.

Baylis John Fletcher

"Wilderness was a source of great joy to the cowboy"

1898–1912

In 1879, twenty-year-old Baylis John Fletcher helped drive a herd of longhorn cattle up the Chisholm Trail from Texas to Wyoming. He began an account of his experiences around 1898 and completed it shortly before his death in 1912. Fletcher's narrative, *Up the Trail in '79*, has, according to Wayne Gard, "a freshness that bespeaks close observation, a sharp memory, and better than ordinary ability in expression." Unlike Siringo's and James's accounts, Fletcher's is history once removed.

On the morning of April 11, a supreme moment for us, we started up the trail to Cheyenne, Wyoming. To gather the cattle in the pasture into one great herd took up the forenoon. In the afternoon we made only about five miles, bedding our cattle that night just south of Victoria, near the Guadalupe River. On the following morning we forded the river, which was low.

When we were passing through the streets of Victoria, a lady, fearful that the cattle would break down her fence and ruin her roses, ran out to the pickets and, waving her bonnet frantically at the cattle, stampeded those in front. With a dull roar, they charged back upon the rear of the herd, and but for the discreet management of boss Arnett, heavy damage to city property would have resulted.

From Baylis John Fletcher, *Up the Trail in '79* (ed. by Wayne Gard, Norman, University of Oklahoma Press, 1968), 16–30, 45–54. Reprinted by permission of the publisher. The explanatory notes to this edition have been omitted.

"Give way at all street crossings and let the cattle have room," he shouted as he galloped about, giving orders to save the City of Roses from a disaster.

We complied quickly and soon had half a dozen residence blocks surrounded by excited and infuriated cattle. Soon they became so confused that the stampede was ended. We gave their fears time to subside, then drove them quietly out of the city without doing any serious damage.

On the second night, when we were camped near the source of Spring Creek, a real midnight stampede occurred. All hands were called to the saddle, and it was near dawn before we could return to our pallets for rest. We proceeded to the north and, in a few days, reached the mouth of Peach Creek, north of Cuero, where we paid for the privilege of watering in the big Kokernot pasture.

Here water was procured in the Guadalupe River, and we stopped on its banks to rest our cattle and eat dinner. While grazing the cattle along the bank of the river, we discovered a big alligator idly floating on the water's surface. All hands were attracted by the strange sight and began shouting at the big saurian, who protected himself by sinking out of sight in the turbid waters.

After dinner Joe Felder took off his boots and washed his feet in the river. Then he sat on the root of a big tree facing the stream and fell asleep. Manuel García, our cook, with that levity characteristic of the Mexican, conceived a practical joke. Throwing a log so that it fell into the river just in front of the sleeping Joe, he shouted, "Alligator!" In a quick effort to rise, Joe slipped into the river, going entirely under and rising by the side of the floating log, which he mistook for the alligator. He screamed for help, and stake ropes were thrown him, which he seized frantically, to be drawn out, as he thought, from the jaws of death. His disgust was profound when he discovered that he was escaping only from a rotten log.

On the following night we bedded our cattle in a short, wide lane between high rail fences a few miles east of Gonzales. This was a thickly settled region, timbered with a variety of oaks, and the surface was covered with gravel. My shift at guard duty was the last in the night, and at about two A.M., Sam Allen, Carteman García, and I were called to go on herd. Allen and I were stationed at the east end of the lane, while the Mexican guarded the other end. The night was frosty, and as the cattle seemed to be sleeping soundly, Sam and I dismounted and built a fire of dry branches by which to warm. At first we would warm by turns and ride time about. But everything was so still that we became careless and both dismounted at the fire, where we began to spin yarns. As the bright fire lit up the scene, it was beautiful to behold. Two thousand cattle rested quietly, lying down and chewing their cuds.

Suddenly there was a loud and ominous roar, while a cloud of dust obscured our vision.

"Stampede!" shouted Sam as he let loose his bridle reins and sprang behind an oak, which he hugged with both hands. I did not have time to turn Happy Jack loose but threw my arms around Allen on the side of the tree opposite the herd. We were none too quick, for now the horns of the stampeding bovines were raking the bark from the opposite side of the oak as they rushed madly past us. It was a moment of supreme terror, but only a moment. In less time than it takes to relate it, the cattle had passed us and, mounting Happy Jack, I was in full pursuit.

I soon overtook the cattle, pressed on past them, and turned their leaders back. They now formed a circle, where they milled in one great wheel, revolving with almost lightning velocity. By holding them in this mill, I soon had them confused, and they began to bellow to one another. I had learned that these were welcome sounds in a stampede. As soon as the bellowing becomes general, the run begins to subside. Of course, such a revolving wheel cannot be stopped suddenly. The momentum they have acquired makes it necessary to slow down the cattle gradually, or else the ones that stopped first would be trampled to death.

I now heard a voice shouting, "Stay with them, Fletcher." In a moment I was joined by Mr. Snyder, riding one of the wagon horses bareback and with a blind bridle. "Where is Sam?" he asked. But I did not know.

We soon had the cattle quiet, and as it now was about dawn, we drove them back to the bed ground. I learned from Mr. Snyder that something had frightened the cattle in about the middle of the lane where we had bedded them and that I was holding only a part of the herd, the remainder having run out of the other end of the lane past García. Thinking that the whole herd had gone that way, the cowboys had all gone to the aid of García, but when Allen and I were missed, Mr. Snyder had gone in search of us. When Allen's horse was found loose with the saddle on, it was supposed that the horse had fallen with him as he rode out ahead of the cattle and that he had narrowly escaped being trampled to death.

We did not confess until long afterward that we had been caught off our horses by the stampede and that Allen had let his horse go. Such admissions were not expected on the trail. After getting the fragments of our herd together, we strung them out in a thin line, and as they passed a certain point, the cattle were counted. It was found that we were about one hundred head short. That many evidently had escaped in the stampede.

While we were discussing the feasibility of recovering the lost cattle, four hard-looking citizens rode up and said. "Had a stampede last night, did you?" We answered in the affirmative. Then the strangers offered their services to help put the cattle back in the herd. Their offer was to bring in all they could for one dollar per head. Mr. Snyder then offered them fifty cents per head, to which they readily agreed. It seemed plain to us that these accommodating gentry had stampeded our herd for this revenue.

They were joined by recruits, and during the day they delivered sixty cattle bearing our road brand. We still were forty short, but time was precious. Mr. Snyder said that the missing ones would go back to the range near Victoria and be gathered there for his account and that we must proceed. Later our own scouts brought in about twenty additional renegades, so that we were only about twenty short when we started forward on the following day.

Moving a large herd through a timbered country was attended with many difficulties. Sometimes a stubborn brute would take to a thicket and fight with wild fury any puncher who tried to dislodge him. In a rocky thicket near Plum Creek one old cow took refuge, and when Poinsett Barton entered on foot to drive her out, she made a desperate lunge to gore him. Barton hurled a stone, striking her in the forehead. Her skull was crushed, and she fell dead. Barton was brought before the boss for killing a cow, but he pleaded self-defense and was acquitted, with a warning not to place himself again in such a position as to make the death of a cow necessary to protect his life.

Suitable bed grounds were difficult to find on this part of the trail. We made use of a line of picket corrals which enterprising residents had erected, and regular herders were stationed around the big pen to watch that the cattle did not escape. For awhile all was quiet, but late in the night the herd stampeded and broke down the fence, giving us another night in the saddle for all hands.

In this stampede, which was on a Saturday night, I lost my hat. On the following morning we came to a country store just south of Lockhart. I called at the home of the merchant and asked him if he kept hats. He said he did. Then I told him of my predicament and asked him to sell me one. He replied that he was sorry for me but that under no circumstances would he sell a hat on the Sabbath. I implored him, speaking of "the ox in the ditch," but he was inexorable in his determination. So I had to ride all day bareheaded. On the next day we arrived at Lockhart, where I rode into town and bought a hat.

The weather in the spring of 1879 was extremely dry. The supply of water along the trail was so scant that often we had to fill our barrel for drinking water from tanks, as the dirty ponds made by the damming of ravines were called. Since this water was contaminated, we were attacked by sickness in the camp. I had fever several days but kept it secret from fear of being sent home.

Anderson Pickett, a Negro Mr. Snyder took along as his servant, came to me one night while I was on herd and said, "Look heah, boy, I know youse sick, ain't yer?"

"Yes," I said. "I'm sick tonight."

"Den you des' let me herd in yo' place. You des' lay down here under dis here mesquite tree, an' I wakes you up 'fo' day." I was too sick to refuse the proffered aid. Dismounting, I gave the reins of old Happy Jack to Anderson, who faithfully did my guard duty until dawn, waking me as promised in time to prevent detection. This relief was of great benefit to me.

We forded the Colorado River at old Webberville, a few miles below Austin. As we drove our cattle across the river, we heard the booming of a cannon in the direction of the capital city. It was April 21, and the people were celebrating the anniversary of the battle of San Jacinto, which had changed the course of Texas history just forty-three years earlier.

We camped near Manor, where I went to a physician and had a

prescription filled. My fever, however, continued to rise every day, and my legs were so swollen that I had to split the uppers of my boots to get them on. My condition was such that I could no longer conceal it. And now it began to rain. All night long the rain poured in torrents. We had reached Brushy Creek north of Manor and near Hutto Station. The pain from inflammatory rheumatism in my ankles was excruciating. We forded Brushy at Rice's Crossing, and Mr. Snyder, learning of my condition, told the faithful Anderson to take me to some farmhouse where I could be cared for and kept dry.

The Negro did his best to comply, but every application for shelter was refused, until we became discouraged. I thought I should have to give up and die of exposure in the cold, blinding April rain. But Anderson persevered. "Yonder is a little rent house," said he. "Mebbe-so we kin git you in dar." Sure enough, the poor renter had not the heart to drive me away. My host and hostess, who had recently married, received me kindly.

Anderson explained that I was one of Tom Snyder's cowboys and that I was sick. The big young fellow said, "Bring him in. We have only one room and are not fixed to entertain, but I have been on the trail myself, and I can't turn off a sick puncher in this rain." I was helped into the cabin as Anderson led my horse away.

Seeing how I was suffering, the tender-hearted young woman burst into tears. "Take our bed, and we will sit up for you," she said.

"No," said I, "just spread my blanket and slicker on the floor. That's all the bed I need."

That night, when all was still and I was supposed to be asleep, I overheard my case discussed by my hosts. "Oh, goodness, John! The boy can't live. Oh, it's awful to be sick on the trail. We could not turn him off to die in this rain. Do you think he will live?"

"You can't tell anything about it, Lucy," came the deep drawl of the husband. "I have been mighty sick on the trail, but I never died. We must do our duty and take care of him until he dies or gets better. That's all we can do."

The cabin had a fireplace, and my host kept a fire all night near my feet. The next morning I felt much improved, but my feet were so swollen that I could not put on my boots. A hot foot bath reduced the swelling, and in the afternoon I was able to sit up. Reaction was now so favorable that on the second morning, at my request, my host carried me on one of his horses to our camp. He refused to accept any pay for my entertainment.

The rainstorm had passed away, and the sun was shining when I rejoined our outfit. Mr. Snyder said I must go home on a sick discharge, as I would not be able to endure the hardships of the trail. I begged him not to dismiss me. He finally agreed to try me awhile longer but told Mr. Arnett to discharge me when we reached Fort Worth if I were not well. My health, however, gave me no more trouble.

Sam Allen, Andy Marcus, and John Ledbetter quit the outfit at Hutto, where new men were hired to take their places. Mr. Snyder also went back to his home at Liberty Hill, turning over the entire responsibility of the trip to our foreman, George Arnett. His faithful Negro, Anderson Pickett, also left us, finding work with a drove of saddle horses bound for Wyoming.

We forded the San Gabriel River near Jonah, a few miles east of Georgetown. Crossing Possum Creek, we followed the Belton road to a bridge on the Lampasas River. Fearing to risk the bridge, we made a detour of several miles and crossed the stream at Saul's Mill. Just as the leaders of our herd came opposite the mill, they took fright at the noise of the machinery and rushed back on the rear cattle. For half an hour the whole herd milled on the bank before we could force them to cross the stream.

Our next camp was on Salado Creek near the village of Salado. There, on the night of May 4, we were caught in a hailstorm that made our cattle drift badly. The severe hail lasted only a few moments, but our heads and shoulders were bruised by the falling ice, and it was many hours before we could quiet the excited cattle. We found the next day that a few miles north of us the hail was so severe that birds, rabbits, and domestic fowls were beaten to death and many crops destroyed. During the hail our saddle horses had stampeded, and we found on taking stock the next morning that two horses were missing. I was detailed to hunt for them and to follow the herd, which crossed the Leon River at Belton. I found only one of the runaways, and by hard riding I overtook the herd that night.

We now entered a more broken country among the hills of McLennan County. We passed to the west of Waco, entering Bosque County at Valley Mills. While camped on Steele's Creek in Bosque

County, we had one of the biggest stampedes of the entire trip. That night a coyote was seen to enter the bed ground of the herd, frightening the cattle and causing them to run. The country was open, and the only loss we suffered was that of a much-needed night's rest. We halted here a day or two to look for a saddle horse that had escaped from Poinsett Barton with a long stake rope attached to it. It was the best horse allotted to him and never was recovered. Perhaps it became entangled by the stake rope in the thickets which covered the hills in that section and perished from starvation.

We were now having a great deal of trouble finding pasturage for our cattle. As long as we kept to the plain beaten trail, we were not molested. But the moment we turned aside to graze our cattle, the settlers came to us, claimed the land upon which our herd was grazing, and ordered us to get off the grass. Under the law, we had to comply quickly or sustain an action for damages. We often doubted the ownership claimed to the grazing lands, but as we had no time to investigate titles, the only safe thing we could do was to move on. We crossed the Brazos River at the old mountain village of Kimball and passed through Johnson County just west of Cleburne. We now had a delightful stretch of prairie, sparsely settled, until we neared Fort Worth. Grass was abundant, and we were rarely molested while seeking forage for our herd.

Fort Worth, with a population of about ten thousand, was then the terminus of the Texas and Pacific Railway and was the last trading point where we could buy supplies on the trail until we should reach Dodge City, Kansas. We were given a day of rest, and, dividing the hands into two shifts, Mr. Arnett said he would allow each of us half a day in town. He planned to buy provisions to last two months. By the Chisholm Trail it was five hundred miles from Fort Worth to Dodge.

Solicitors from the big grocery stores of Fort Worth met us on horseback several miles from the city, bringing such gifts as bottles of whisky and boxes of fine cigars. Steve Pointer, known as Shug in our outfit, was the oldest cowpuncher we had, and looking older than Mr. Arnett, he often was mistaken for the boss. Frequently the mistake worked to Shug's advantage, though there would come a time when he regretted that he did not look more like a cowpuncher.

The drummers from Fort Worth all wanted to see the boss, who was purchasing agent for the outfit, and by previous arrangement Shug played his part well, accepting a box of fine cigars, some whisky, and other blandishments. Mr. Arnett quietly trailed the cattle while Shug stopped to talk with the drummers. After he thought Shug had accepted all that was due him, Will Bower rode swiftly to the rear and shouted to the erstwhile boss, "Shug, the boss says come on, you lazy cuss, and get to work, or he'll turn you off at Fort Worth." It then dawned upon the solicitors that they had been buncoed and that they would need a new supply of gifts to corral the real boss when he was identified. Shug became angry at Will for interrupting his game and made some uncomplimentary remarks.

Leaving Fort Worth, we followed the trail north, passing in sight of Decatur to our left and Saint Jo to our right, crossing parts of Wise, Denton, Cook, and Montague counties. Since Montague was a border county, we were told that we could wear side arms without fear of arrest, so every cowpuncher who had a six-shooter buckled it on just to enjoy the privilege of carrying a weapon.

As we passed a farmhouse near Saint Jo, a fine Shorthorn bull broke out of a pasture and joined our herd. We cut him repeatedly, but he followed on about a mile to a point where we bedded our cattle for the night. The next morning the indignant owner came to us and demanded we take his bull back to the pasture, threatening to prosecute us if we did not. We advised him to take the animal back with him, but he haughtily refused to do so and threatened to have us arrested for carrying pistols in Montague County. We promised that we would carry the animal no farther but did not agree to take him back. He rode away in a great rage, continuing his threats. After he had gone we roped the bull, threw him down, hogged his feet together with strong cords, and left him lying on the ground as we moved our herd down the valley of Farmer's Creek to Spanish Fort, where we were to cross the Red River and enter the Indian Territory.

On or about the first day of June we came in sight of the Red River Valley, beyond which we could see the Indian Territory. The country ahead was then a wilderness, without a human habitation in view of the Chisholm Trail to the line of Kansas, nearly three hundred miles away by the meanderings of our route.

As we were gazing upon this distant prospect, several well-mounted horsemen rode up, and their leader informed Mr. Arnett that he was a cattle inspector, whose duty it was to inspect carefully every herd crossing the northern boundary of Texas, cutting out any estrays that might be in the herd not bearing the road brand of the outfit. We were instructed to string the cattle out in a line, so that they might be passed one or two at a time between the inspector and one of his assistants, to be examined carefully as to their ownership.

Four or five little dogies, as poor little orphan yearlings were called, had escaped our vigilance in cutting out strays, and they were taken out of the herd by the inspector and turned over to his assistants. After the inspection was over, Mr. Arnett paid the inspector his per capita fee for examining the herd, which in our case amounted to about seventy-five dollars.

Having undergone this inspection, our herd was given a clean bill of health, and we were permitted to take the cattle across the Red River, which at this point was low and easily forded. The prospect of entering an uninhabited wilderness was a source of great joy to the cowboys. Civilization and cattle trailing were not congenial, and we had been greatly annoyed in the settled districts of Texas. Depending entirely on free grass for forage for our cattle and horses, we had constantly come in collision with the farmers, who wanted the grass for their domestic animals.

We were not alone on the trail. The big drive northward was at its height, and that spring there were probably 500,000 cattle and horses moving up the one universal trail from South Texas. Often we had been driven by angry men, with ferocious dogs, from tract to tract of grazing land, but our movements were so deliberate that the cattle got enough to live upon. The Indian Territory was the cowpuncher's paradise. Now we would have no more lanes, no more obstructing fences, but one grand expanse of free grass. It was a delightful situation to contemplate.

Our Mexican cook was unfortunate in crossing the Red River. He stopped his wagon in the middle of the stream to fill his water barrel. While he was doing so, the wagon settled to the axles in the yielding quicksands. The oxen were unable to move. Manuel began to beat them with his whip, and the oxen turned quickly to one side, breaking the tongue out of the wagon and leaving it bogged in the

A Cherokee Outlet cowboy prepares for a roping competition. The soles of his boots are evidence that he has seen better days.

One cowboy gives another a haircut at a line camp on the Matador Ranch in Texas. A towel and brush hang by the door, near the precarious washstand. A saddle and other gear occupy the foreground.

After breakfast cowboys on roundup head for the remuda, leaving the camp in disarray. Note the plates stacked on the ground beneath the chuck box and the kerosene lamps hanging from the wagon tail.

Cowboys catching their saddle horses from a remuda in the Texas-Oklahoma panhandle area in the 1890's. The photographer caught two of the cowboys with their ropes in the air.

Caught and saddled, a cow pony was still not ready for a day's work. Each morning the cowboy had to re-establish his authority. Here a cowboy loses his hat in the process.

Cowboys eat while ground-hitched horses wait, saddled and ready.

A Matador herd moves over a trail marked by wagon ruts.

Bringing up the drags.

Bulldogging demonstrated for the camera. The photograph is more instructive on the subject of the cult of the masculine than on the techniques of cowboying.

river. We went to his rescue and, cutting a cottonwood pole, lashed it with ropes to the broken wagon tongue. But the team could not move it. Finally, after we borrowed two additional yokes of oxen from a neighboring outfit, the six big steers hauled the wagon out of the river. A dried cowhide suspended under the wagon like a hammock and known as the caboose or possum-belly held kindling wood, stake pins for our horses, and other implements for use on the trail. All of the contents that would float were lost, drifting away upon the reddish waters of the river....

We crossed the Cimarron again right at the line of Kansas. We were informed that this was the last water we should find until we reached the Arkansas at Dodge City, more than a hundred miles away. The waters of the Cimarron were good at this point, and we watered our herd freely before starting the long drive. We filled our water barrel to the brim, but we started out for a hundred miles without stock water. We had not been averaging more than twelve miles a day, but now we must exceed that rate or our animals would die of thirst before we could reach the Arkansas.

Four days later, on the glorious Fourth of July, we came in sight of the Arkansas River. We had lost no cattle, but they were staggering along in a line for at least five miles up and down the trail. The stronger had outtraveled the weaker, and the herd was pulled in two, forming two distinct droves. Fortunately, there had been showers in the Arkansas Valley south of Dodge City, forming small ponds that enabled the cattle gradually to slake their thirst before they reached the river. Otherwise, we might have lost some cattle from overdrinking.

During the time that Mr. Arnett was disabled, there had been a serious difficulty between some of our men and the two Mexicans, which nearly resulted in a shooting affray. Having reduced the number of our cattle by the delivery of three hundred beeves at Fort Supply, we did not need so many hands, and, to prevent further trouble, Mr. Arnett decided to discharge the Garcías at Dodge City. They were tired of the trip and were more than willing to quit. So the chili-eaters, as some cowboys called them, were permitted to resign. Presenting a letter of credit from Mr. Snyder, Mr. Arnett procured the money to pay their wages, and on July 5, I was sent with them to the Atchison, Topeka and Santa Fe station, where they bought tickets to Galveston. I then returned to camp, fording the Arkansas River at the old cow trail.

We now got into trouble through ignorance of Kansas customs. We had never traveled in a country with herd laws. Not dreaming that any men would try to grow a crop of grain without fencing his land, we let our whole herd of 1,700 cattle invade the wheat field of a homesteader. He drove us out with dogs and lurid oaths, but when he was informed of our ignorance, he laughed and said he would excuse us this time but that we must not repeat the experiment.

We bought a fresh supply of provisions at Dodge City, including a keg of pickles. During the entire trip we had tasted no vegetables other than beans or "prairie strawberries" as some called them, and when the pickles were opened, the men would eat nothing else until they were all devoured.

Dodge was said to be the wickedest town in the West at that time, but we saw little of its wickedness. Our stay in town was limited to a few hours each, and that during the day. No cowpuncher was permitted to stay in town at night. Among the curiosities I saw at the station were great piles of buffalo bones awaiting shipment. They were enormous, with the skulls of many of the big bulls still decorated with the short, thick horns peculiar to the buffalo.

After our shopping was done, we forded the Arkansas River and kept well to the north through western Kansas. The plains were high now, and all watercourses flowed through deep canyons. There were scattered settlements made by homesteaders. The settlers lived chiefly in dugouts, excavations in the sides of canyons, with roofs thatched with grass and then covered with turf. Sometimes we saw houses built of prairie sod as it was turned by the plow and cut in sections like building stones. We were told that in these semi-arid regions sod houses lasted for years.

On one occasion, as we were guiding our weary herd along the trail, the big steers that always led the herd saw a heap of earth and ran bellowing to it. They began to paw it with their forefeet and to toss the turf with their horns. We were unaware that they were destroying a human habitation until a woman came running out from an opening in the ground and fighting the steers frantically with her sun-bonnet. When she called on us to drive the cattle away, we hastened to the rescue, but it was too late. The roof of the dugout was caved in and the frontier home ruined. Again we pleaded ignorance, but with no more success than at Dodge City. The woman was greatly exasperated by the partial destruction of her dugout. We offered our services to help rebuild it, but she disdainfully declined them, declaring that persons who were so ignorant as to allow their cattle to destroy the dugout could do little toward repairing it. We were extremely sorry, but we could not gain her forgiveness.

Passing on, we were met by a band of homesteaders mounted on mules and brood mares, all bareback and some barefoot. They approached us in a body and informed us that we must turn to the west, as they had settled on the trail directly north from us and would not allow any Texas cattle to be driven through their settlement. Texas fever, they declared, scattered Texas-fever germs, and the fever would kill their domestic cattle. There was no alternative but to yield to their wishes. We were not prepared to make a forcible invasion of Kansas but must do as directed. So, turning out of our trail, we made a detour of about fifteen miles to go around this settlement.

Not far from this place we found a lone herder running a trail hospital. From several herds, crippled and disabled cattle had been cut out into a hospital bunch and left with this young man to be cared for until they should be able to travel. I was surprised to find that the lonely herder was my old neighbor, Nicholas Branch of Bagdad, Williamson County, Texas. Nick Branch was noted for his faithfulness in every position in which he was placed. I had always admired this trait of his character, but I did not envy him the responsibility of serving as nurse to a drove of lame cattle. He had several horses at his disposal, and he probably arranged with some squatter for his board.

A little farther on, we saw a pathetic scene on the trail. Beside the carcass of a dead horse was a newly made grave. An examination showed that the animal had been killed by lightning. Evidently the thunderbolt had carried instant death to both horse and rider. There was no one to explain, but no explanation was needed. Some Texas cowboy on duty had cashed in—had been killed by lightning and was buried beside the body of his faithful horse. Wolves had nearly devoured the animal's carcass but had not molested the cowboy's grave. There on the wild plains of western Kansas he had been buried, without a woman's tears, without a single tribute of flowers, and doubtless without a coffin. Perhaps a slicker was his only winding sheet. We never learned anything of his history, but here was a solemn admonition to the cowboy that death lurked in the storms that swept over the plains with vivid flashes of lightning.

We now crossed the Kansas Pacific Railroad at Buffalo Parks station, noted as the place where two bandits of the famous Big Springs train robbery had been killed less than two years earlier. They were trying to escape with their booty from Big Springs, Nebraska, when they were killed in a fight with United States troops. In company with Sam Bass, who later was killed by Texas Rangers at Round Rock, Texas, where he planned to rob a bank, and with three other desperadoes, they had stopped the Union Pacific express at Big Springs. They looted the express car, making a rich haul of sixty thousand dollars in twenty-dollar gold pieces being shipped east from California.

On the afternoon of the first day after leaving Buffalo Parks station, we met a man riding across the plain, stopping at intervals to survey the horizon with a field glass. His movements excited our curiosity, and when he came up to us and asked whether we had seen any Indians, we became deeply interested. He said it was rumored that the Cheyennes had left their reservation at Fort Supply in the Indian Territory and had gone on the warpath. It was said that they were following the cow trail to their hunting grounds in Dakota. The rumor further credited them with having killed and scalped a number of settlers in western Kansas. We knew that during the summer of 1878, just one year before, the Cheyennes had made a raid through Kansas and Nebraska, massacring many homesteaders. Later in the afternoon we met several more scouts who told the same story as the lone horseman.

Just before sunset we entered a deep canyon through which flowed a small stream which we were told was a tributary of the Republican River. While we were selecting a camping spot for the night, another scout arrived, claiming to have recent news. He said that the Cheyennes in a large body had crossed the railroad just west of Buffalo Parks on the preceding night and that they were headed north. They must be hiding in some of the deep canyons in our immediate vicinity. He cautioned us to look out for a raid that night. We found some dry driftwood along the creek, and for the first time in many weeks we built a big wood fire by which to eat our evening meal. The cattle had been bedded down about a quarter of a mile farther up the canyon, and three men were guarding them.

As we were quietly eating our supper, these three cowboys dashed up to our camp and said that a large body of horsemen, presumably Indians, were crossing the canyon just above our camp. George Arnett sprang to his feet and called for three volunteers to go with him to reconnoiter. Poinsett Barton, Dick Russell, and I joined him. Arming ourselves, we rode quietly by the dim starlight to the sleeping cattle, then beyond them to the west for half a mile, but we saw no man. We rode up the steep canyon walls to the level plain and halted while Mr. Arnett, who was an old Indian fighter, dismounted and put his ear to the ground. He heard the distant tramping of a large body of horses. We all dismounted then and scanned the horizon of the level plain.

Silhouetted against the northern sky, we saw what appeared to be a large body of horses, or horsemen, rapidly receding in the distant gloom. They might be renegade savages, but if so they had passed us and it would be madness to pursue them. So we followed the rim of the canyon until we were opposite our campfire. Just as we turned to descend, we heard the sound of horses' hoofs and we saw the dim outline of a man on horseback chasing our saddle horses. "Don't shoot!" shouted Mr. Arnett as one of our number brought his carbine to bear on the rider. "I think it's Al Cochran driving the horses." On returning to camp, we found that he was right. The boy had driven the horses up to the wagon.

After reporting the result of our reconnaissance, Mr. Arnett said, "Now, boys, I don't think there is a particle of danger tonight, for the strangers, whoever they are, have crossed the creek and are rapidly leaving us. They will not return. But if any of you are uneasy, we can safely leave the herd and the wagon and go up the canyon a mile or so and remain concealed for the night. The cattle will not run off, and there are no range cattle to mix with them. If no Indians come, the cattle and horses will be safe. If they do come in such force as reported, we shall be powerless to resist them. I do not believe all these Indian tales, but I leave it to you as to what we shall do tonight."

After some discussion, during which I could not help recalling some of Aunt Ellen's stories of Indian massacres, we took a vote and, by an overwhelming majority, decided to leave camp for the night. So we replenished the campfire and filed quietly away on our night horses up the canyon of the creek. Finding a secluded spot hedged in by wild currant bushes, we dismounted and placed a sentinel on guard at the top of the canyon's side. We staked our horses with their saddles on. At regular intervals during the night the sentinel was relieved of his picket duty. Nothing disturbed the silence on the plain during the night except the occasional howl of a coyote.

On the following morning we returned to camp, where we found nothing molested. The cattle had scattered a little, but soon we had them rounded up and ready for the trail. There was no trace of savages. After breakfast we resumed our march up the trail. We soon came to a trail leading to the garrison at Oberlin. It was lined with homesteaders and their families, all in a state of panic from the Indian tales. Some of the women and girls were weeping and some were laughing, but all were flying for their lives to get within the shelter of the soldiers' guns at Oberlin. Scouts were riding over the plains with field glasses, trying in vain to locate the Indians. For several days the panic continued. As we approached the dugouts of the homesteaders, we found them deserted. We no longer had any trouble from settlers who might try to turn us away from our course. No one molested us. In fact, the people seemed glad for our presence. But where were the bloodthirsty Cheyennes?

At last we came to the south prong of Sappa River. There, grazing in the valley, was a herd of about eight hundred horses and a full outfit of cowboys herding them. The outfit was from Texas, and the horses were being trailed to Ogallala, Nebraska, to supply the demand for cow ponies on the big ranches. The boss of the horse herd approached us with a bland smile. After exchanging greetings, he asked, "Seen any Indians?"

"No," we replied, "but we have heard of them every day. What does all this mean?"

"Well," said the horse driver, "we were so harassed by the

settlers driving us from place to place that we had to resort to some expedient to make us welcome intruders. They would not let us pass through their settlements and would not let us rest to graze our horses, so we had to do something. We began making night drives and putting out Indian reports. The raid of last year was fresh in memory, and all we had to do to depopulate the plains was to start Indian tales. In our night drives during the dark of the moon, we were mistaken for a strong band of Cheyennes. We are the only Indians in western Kansas, but please keep mum. If they get onto our joke, they will come back and hang us every one. We passed your herd one night on the north prong of the Solomon River. Did you take us for Indians, too?"

It was all plain to us now. We were innocent of the trickery, but we had shared in the benefits of the panic. The unscrupulous old frontiersman who bossed the horse herd knew the source of that hospitality characteristic of border inhabitants when there is danger of savage foes. He had succeeded in making himself welcome by exciting the gravest fears among people unused to the dangers of frontier life. They were all settlers from the East and were easily thrown into a panic by a suggestion of Indians. He had resorted to a heroic treatment for selfishness and had worked a marvelous cure. But, as he said, the secret must be kept until he was at a safe distance from the victims of this faked scare.

Alfred Henry Lewis

"He becomes deeply and famously drunk"

1902

A Cleveland, Ohio, attorney turned newspaperman, Alfred Henry Lewis spent time in New Mexico and Arizona and became popular through his collections of range stories narrated by a character known as the Old Cattleman. Lewis wove fiction on a fabric of fact and seems to have known whereof he spoke. In the following passage, taken from his *Wolfville Nights*, Lewis set out to introduce the reader to the subject of cowboys.

While the farms in their westward pushing do not diminish the cattle, they reduce the cattleman and pinch off much that is romantic and picturesque. Between the farm and the wire fence, the cowboy, as once he flourished, has been modified, subdued, and made partially to disappear. In the good old days of the Jones and Plummer trail there were no wire fences, and the sullen farmer had not yet arrived. Your cowboy at that time was a person of thrill and consequence. He wore a broad-brimmed Stetson hat, and all about it a rattlesnake skin by way of band, retaining head and rattles. This was to be potent against headaches—a malady, by the way, which swept down no cowboy save in hours emergent of a spree. In such case the snake cure didn't cure. The hat was retained in defiance of winds, by a leathern cord caught about the back of the head, not

From Alfred Henry Lewis, *Wolfville Nights* (New York, Frederick A. Stokes Company, 1902), 7–15.

under the chin. This cord was beautiful with a garniture of three or four perforated poker chips, red, yellow, and blue.

There are sundry angles of costume where the dandyism of a cowboy of spirit and conceit may acquit itself; these are hatband, spurs, saddle, and leggins. I've seen hatbands made of braided gold and silver filigree; they were from Santa Fe, and always in the form of a rattlesnake, with rubies or emeralds or diamonds for eyes. Such gauds would cost from four hundred to two thousand dollars. Also, I've encountered a saddle which depleted its proud owner a round twenty-five hundred dollars. It was of finest Spanish leather, stamped and spattered with gold bosses. There was gold-capping on the saddle horn, and again on the circle of the cantle. It was a dream of a saddle, made at Paso del Norte; and the owner had it cinched upon a bronco dear at twenty dollars. One couldn't have sold the pony for a stack of white chips in any faro game of that neighbourhood (Las Vegas) and they were all crooked games at that.

Your cowboy dandy frequently wears wrought steel spurs, inlaid with silver and gold; price, anything you please. If he flourish a true Brummel of the plains his leggins will be fronted from instep to belt with the thick pelt, hair outside, of a Newfoundland dog. These "chapps," are meant to protect the cowboy from rain and cold, as well as plum bushes, wire fences and other obstacles inimical, and against which he may lunge while riding headlong in the dark. The hair of the Newfoundland, thick and long and laid the right way, defies the rains; and your cowboy loathes water.

Save in those four cardinals of vanity enumerated, your cowboy wears nothing from weakness; the rest of his outfit is legitimate. The long sharp heels of his boots are there to dig into the ground and hold fast to his mother earth while roping on foot. His gay pony when "roped" of a frosty morning would skate him all across and about the plains if it were not for these heels. The buckskin gloves tied in one of the saddle strings are used when roping, and to keep the half-inch manila lariat—or mayhap it's horse-hair or rawhide pleated—from burning his hands. The red silken sash one was wont aforetime to see knotted about his waist, was used to hogtie and hold down the big cattle when roped and thrown. The sash—strong, soft and close—could be tied more tightly, quickly, surely than anything besides. In these days, with wire pastures and branding pens and the fine certainty of modern round-ups and a consequent paucity of mavericks, big cattle are seldom roped; wherefor the sash has been much cast aside.

The saddle-bags or "war-bags,"—also covered of dogskin to match the leggins, and worn behind, not forward of the rider—are the cowboy's official wardrobe wherein he carries his second suit of underclothes, and his other shirt. His handkerchief, red cotton, is loosely knotted about the cowboy's neck, knot to the rear. He wipes the sweat from his brow therewith on those hot Texas days when in a branding pen he "flanks" calves or feeds the fires or handles the irons or stands off the horned indignation of the cows, resentful because of burned and bawling offspring.

It would take two hundred thousand words to tell in half fashion the story of the cowboy. His religion of fatalism, his courage, his rides at full swing in midnight darkness to head and turn and hold a herd stampeded, when a slip on the storm-soaked grass by his unshod pony, or a misplaced prairie-dog hole, means a tumble, and a tumble means that a hundred and fifty thousand dollars worth of cattle, with hoofs like chopping knives, will run over him and make him look and feel and become as dead as a cancelled postage stamp; his troubles, his joys, his soberness in camp, his drunkenness in town, and his feuds and occasional "gun-plays" are not to be disposed of in a preface. One cannot in such cramped space so much as hit the high places in a cowboy career.

At work on the range and about his camp—for, bar accidents, wherever you find a cowboy you will find a camp—the cowboy is a youth of sober quiet dignity. There is a deal of deep politeness and nothing of epithet, insult or horseplay where everybody wears a gun.

There are no folk inquisitive on the ranges. No one asks your name. If driven by stress of conversation to something akin to it the cowboy will say: "What may I call you, sir?" And he's as careful to add the "sir," as he is to expect it in return. You are at liberty to select what name you prefer. Where you hail from? where going? why? are queries never put. To look at the brand on your pony—you, a stranger—is a dangerous vulgarity to which no gentleman of the Panhandle or any other region of pure southwestern politeness would stoop. And if you wish to arouse an instant combination of hate, suspicion and contempt in the bosom of a cowboy you have but to stretch forth your artless Eastern hand and ask: "Let me look at your gun."

Cowboys on the range or in the town are excessively clannish. They never desert each other, but stay and fight and die and storm a jail and shoot a sheriff if needs press, to rescue a comrade made captive in their company. Also they care for each other when sick or injured, and set one another's bones when broken in the falls and tumbles of their craft. On the range the cowboy is quiet, just and peaceable. There are neither women nor cards nor rum about the cow camps. The ranches and the boys themselves banish the two latter; and the first won't come. Women, cards and whiskey, the three war causes of the West, are confined to the towns.

Those occasions when cattle are shipped and the beef-herds, per consequence, driven to the shipping point become the only times when the cowboy sees the town. In such hours he blooms and lives fully up to his opportunity. He has travelled perhaps two hundred miles and has been twenty days on the trail, for cattle may only be driven about ten miles a day; he has been up day and night and slept half the time in the saddle; he has made himself hoarse singing "Sam Bass" and "The Dying Ranger" to keep the cattle quiet and stave off stampedes; he has ridden ten ponies to shadows in his twenty days of driving, wherefore, and naturally, your cowboy feels like relaxing.

There would be as many as ten men with each beef-herd; and the herd would include about five thousand head. There would be six "riders," divided into three watches to stand night guard over the herd and drive it through the day; there would be two "hoss hustlers," to hold the eighty or ninety ponies, turn and turn about, and carry them along with the herd; there would be the cook, with four mules and the chuck wagon; and lastly there would be the herd-boss, a cow expert he, and at the head of the business.

Once the herd is off his hands and his mind at the end of the drive, the cowboy unbuckles and reposes himself from his labours. He becomes deeply and famously drunk. Hungering for the excitement of play he collides amiably with faro and monte and what other deadfalls are rife of the place. Never does he win; for the games aren't arranged that way. But he enjoys himself; and his losses do not prey on him.

Sated with faro bank and monte—they can't be called games of chance, the only games of chance occurring when cowboys engage with each other at billiards or pool—sated, I say, with faro and Mexican monte, and exuberant of rum, which last has regular quick renewal, our cowboy will stagger to his pony, swing into the saddle, and with gladsome whoops and an occasional outburst from his six shooter directed toward the heavens, charge up and down the street. This last amusement appeals mightily to cowboys too drunk to walk. For, be it known, a gentleman may ride long after he may not walk.

If a theatre be in action and mayhap a troop of "Red Stocking Blondes," elevating the drama therein, the cowboy is sure to attend. Also he will arrive with his lariat wound about his body under his coat; and his place will be the front row. At some engaging crisis, such as the "March of the Amazons," having first privily unwound and organised his lariat to that end, he will arise and "rope" an Amazon. This will produce bad language from the manager of the show, and compel the lady to sit upon the stage to the detriment of her wardrobe if no worse, and all to keep from being pulled across the footlights. Yet the exercise gives the cowboy deepest pleasure. Having thus distinguished the lady of his admiration, later he will meet her and escort her to the local dancehall. There, mingling with their frank companions, the two will drink, and loosen the boards of the floor with the strenuous dances of our frontier till daylight does appear.

For the matter of a week, or perchance two—it depends on how fast his money melts—in these fashions will our gentleman of cows engage his hours and expand himself. He will make a deal of noise, drink a deal of whiskey, acquire a deal of what he terms "action"; but he harms nobody, and, in a town toughened to his racket and which needs and gets his money, disturbs nobody.

"Let him whoop it up; he's paying for it, ain't he?" will be the prompt local retort to any inquiry as to why he is thus permitted to disport.

So long as the cowboy observes the etiquette of the town, he will not be molested or "called down" by marshal or sheriff or citizen. There are four things your cowboy must not do. He must not insult a woman; he must not shoot his pistol in a store or bar-room; he must not ride his pony into those places of resort; and as a last proposal he must not ride his pony on the sidewalks. Shooting or riding into bar-rooms is reckoned as dangerous; riding on the sidewalk comes more under the head of insult, and is popularly regarded as a taunting defiance of the town marshal. On such occasions the marshal never fails to respond, and the cowboy is called upon to surrender. If he complies, which to the credit of his horse-sense he commonly does, he is led into brief captivity to be made loose when cooled. Does he resist arrest, there is an explosive rattle of six shooters, a mad scatter-ing of the careful citizenry out of lines of fire, and a cowboy or marshal is added to the host beyond. At the close of the festival, if the marshal still lives he is congratulated; if the cowboy survives he is lynched; if both fall, they are buried with the honours of frontier war; while whatever the event, the communal ripple is but slight and only of the moment, following which the currents of Western exis-tence sweep easily and calmly onward as before.

National Live Stock Association

"No class of men ever was so unfaithfully represented"

1905

If an "official" view of the cowboy exists, it is to be found in the selection that follows, taken from *Prose and Poetry of the Live Stock Industry of the United States*. The book, edited by James W. Freeman, was prepared for the membership of the National Live Stock Association. Drawing upon the works of Emerson Hough, Theodore Roosevelt, and Andy Adams, it argues that the cowboy has generally been misunderstood and describes a life on the range in which only the fittest survived. Considering its publication date and the purpose to which it was put, the book must be viewed as basically nostalgic and essentially self-serving. It preserves what cattlemen thought worth preserving.

One of the groups of temporary "statuary" with which the great Louisiana Purchase Exposition at St. Louis in 1904 was embellished represented four yelling cowboys mounted on galloping "cow-horses" and firing their revolvers in the air—"shooting up the town." No doubt a large majority of the visitors to that incomparable exposition who saw this group regarded it as being truly typical in its representation of the cowboy of the old cattle-trails and of the by-gone days of the open range.

It would seem that no class of men ever was so unfaithfully represented, whether intentionally or unintentionally, and in con-

From James W. Freeman (ed.), *Prose and Poetry of the Live Stock Industry of the United States* (Denver, National Live Stock Historical Association, 1905), I, 548–64.

sequence of this so wrongfully understood and unfairly judged by the people generally, as that of the old-time cowboys has been; and it is to be regretted that this class of western pioneers was figured at this great Exposition in a form so well calculated to lend support to and to perpetuate the mistaken common notions that the general public has concerning these men.

Of the typical cowboy Mr. Emerson Hough, in his most interesting book, "The Story of the Cowboy," says:

"What was really the life of this child of the wild region of America, and what were the conditions of the life that bore him can never be fully known by those who have not seen the West with wide eyes. Those who did not, but who looked superficially and superciliously, remembering only their own surroundings, and forgetting that in the eye of Nature one creature is as good as another if only it prevail where it stands, were content with distorted views of that which they saw about them. Having no perspective in their souls, how could they find it in their eyes? They saw color but not form in these wild men of the wild country. They saw traits but did not see the character beneath them. Seeking to tell of that which they had not seen, they became inaccurate and unjust. Dallying with the pleasant sensation of exciting themes, they became grotesque instead of strong in their handling of them.

"The cowboy was simply a part of the West. He who did not understand the one could never understand the other. Never was any character more misunderstood than he; and so thorough was his misrepresentation that part of the public even to-day will have no other way of looking at him. They see the wide hat and not the honest face beneath it. They remember the wild momentary freaks of man, but forget his lifetime of hard work and patient faithfulness. They insist upon the distorted mask and ask not for the soul beneath it. If we care truly to see the cowboy as he was, and seek to give our wish the dignity of a real purpose, the first intention should be to study the cowboy in connection with his surroundings. Then perhaps we may not fail in our purpose, but come near to seeing him as he actually was, the product of primitive, chaotic, elemental forces, rough, barbarous, and strong. Then we shall love him because at heart each of us is a barbarian, too, and longing for that past the ictus of whose heredity we can never eliminate from out our blood. Then

Cowboys posing after supper. The fourth man from the left is a Negro. The photographic record suggests that Negro cowboys may not have been as prevalent as some historians have indicated.

Cowboys photographed on a ranch near Comstock, Texas, in the 1890's.

A large group of cowboys pauses for the camera during a noon meal. The fourth man from the right displays his revolver while, at the rear of the second wagon, the cook scrubs a pan. The cowboy in the center on the front row seems to be holding a jar containing insect specimens. A pan of biscuits sits near a coffeepot in the foreground.

Cowboys doff their hats for a group portrait.

A Sunday outing on a Woodward County, Oklahoma, ranch. The woman
in the buckboard holds a parasol, and a little girl sits with her doll atop
the chuck wagon, suggesting that the cowboy life was not entirely devoid
of ameliorating influences.

we shall feel him appeal to something hid deep down in our common nature. And this is the way we should look at the cowboy of the passing West; not as a curiosity, but as a product; not as an eccentric driver of horned cattle, but as a man suited to his times."

Theodore Roosevelt, in his "Ranch Life and the Hunting Trail" (1888), bears this testimony to the intrinsic character of the typical cowboy:

"It is utterly unfair to judge the whole class by what a few individuals do in the course of two or three days spent in town, instead of by the long months of weary, honest toil, common to all alike. To appreciate properly his fine, manly qualities, the wild rough rider of the plains should be seen in his own home. There he passes his days, there he does his life-work, there, when he meets death, he faces it as he has faced many other evils, with quiet, uncomplaining fortitude. Brave, hospitable, hardy, and adventurous, he is the grim pioneer of our race; he prepares the way for the civilization from before whose face he must himself disappear. Hard and dangerous though his existence is, it has yet a wild attraction that strongly draws to it his bold, free spirit. He lives in the lonely lands where mighty rivers twist in long reaches between the barren bluffs; where the prairies stretch out into billowy plains of waving grass, girt only by the blue horizon,—plains across whose endless breadth he can steer his course for days and weeks and see neither man to speak to nor hill to break the level; where the glory and the burning splendor of the sunsets kindle the blue vault of heaven and the level brown earth till they merge together in an ocean of flaming fire."

Twenty or twenty-five years ago most through travelers upon the plains railroads seemed to regard the cowboy as a creature indigenous to the range country—the same as the antelope, the coyote, and the prairie "dog," and were even more eager to catch sight of one of the species than they were to see any of those which went on four legs. The people had read about the cowboy, and so they had their ready-made notions as to what he should look like and as to how he should act; and therefore they accepted any broad-hatted, weather-beaten lounger around the railroad stations as a man just in from the cattle-range. If he happened to have a "gun" strapped to him, and could be imagined to be wearing an expression of disappointment because the moment afforded him no occasion for unlimbering his artillery and furiously going into action, he was at once raised to the rank of a "bad man" cowboy, though he may never have seen a herd of cattle on the range, and his character and reputation may have been such that he could not have stayed longer than over-night in any cow-camp in the country; and then only when he had pleaded distress and was kept under surveillance.

Perhaps in no other occupation of men was the theory of the "survival of the fittest" more plainly demonstrated in practice than in the quick weeding out of the weaklings, of the visionary, and of the inherently depraved, among those who undertook the cowboy life. The first to go were those physically unable to stand the labor and hardships of the range. The second, while physically strong, found the life so far different from what they had pictured it that they dropped out as they realized that it was a daily round of duty and work under a code of rules and customs which, though not having the form of statutory law, were in practice almost as rigid as the regulations of an army. For several years after the Civil War a considerable number of the second class turned cowboys, but such men, as a rule, could not stay for long. In the close communion of cowboy life on the trail and the range, where trust, faithfulness, and the spirit of brotherhood and mutual confidence had to be, a man inherently depraved was out of place.

As a class, the cowboys were no such lawless beings as they have so often been represented. They were hardy, fearless, and reckless, products of the conditions by which they were surrounded, but not vicious as a body. Their life was one of hardship, isolation, and self-denial, yet through it all, loyalty to the interests of their employer was steadfast; and whatever might be the privations of their occupation they met and endured them uncomplainingly. Very few of the noted western desperadoes—"professional man-killers"— ever were cowboys or in any way connected with the range-cattle business. These infested the ghastly frontier towns of the cowboy era, for the lonely life of the range was not to their liking.

Truly, it was a lonely life. On the great open ranges the whole outlook soon became one vast, featureless, confusing impression, like that derived from the ocean. Moreover, the general aspect of the plains was, as it still is where the works of men have not disturbed it, one of sadness—even of melancholy. The land seemed to be grieving over something that was lost forever. Then there was the silence of it. This was unlike that of mountain solitudes and different from that of the sea. It was of a kind that does not submit to "description." The effects of the atmosphere of sadness, of the loneliness, and of the unbroken quiet of the vast stretches of the plains became oppressive, burdensome, maddening. No one unfamiliar with them can understand what these effects were. They bore down upon the mind as would a heavy weight upon the body; and a torturing heartache then kept company with a sense of exile. Under the burden of these depressing influences men felt like crying aloud in feeble attempts to break the wall of silence and loneliness by which they were encompassed; and often they did so. In some instances reason was dethroned, for it is a peculiarity of man that he can better endure almost any other condition than that of solitude. But recently a case of insanity from these causes became personally known to the present writer. It was that of a young man engaged in sheep-raising in Wyoming, whose unbalancing plainly was due to the depressing effects of his solitary life on a lonely range. It is doubtful if ever there was a cowboy who did not, at times at least, feel the burden of these influences; and the cattle not uncommonly showed that even they were not immune.

Is it any wonder then that the cowboy who went with a trail-herd to one of the old wild and woolly cowtowns after months, maybe a year, of such isolation as this, "turned loose," as he called it, and even sounded the depths of the iniquities that dominated in these miserable places? or need we be surprised when told that upon his more frequent visits to his nearest grizzly local hamlet he took possession of the place and for a day or so "run" it to suit himself, or tried to? need it seem strange to us that the "attractions" of such aggregations of vice and crime as the old Abilene, or Great Bend City, or Dodge City, demoralized him and brought him low—though they made him a victim more often than they made him a "terror"? Has the reader ever had the experience of sudden relief from some mental strain? has he had the eager feeling that follows the off-casting of a load that has borne him down? or has he ever had the buoyancy of spirit that comes with a return from a sojourn in the wilderness to the haunts of his fellow-men? If so, as to either, probably he may in a measure understand how it came about that the cowboy, fresh from the loneliness of the range or from the drudgery of the trail, when he found himself in the midst of houses and people, "painted the town" in variegated colors and made a fool of himself generally, without necessarily having been a bad man at heart.

While a trace of the savage element still lingers in the blood of most of us, the gregarious instincts of our species are so strong that we are likely to be impelled to "celebrate" in some way the end of any separation from our fellow-creatures that circumstances may have imposed upon us. This is exactly what the cowboy usually undertook to do when he went to town. Perhaps our ways of doing this would not be such as his were, but in the spirit and motive probably there would be little if any difference. As Mr. Roosevelt remarks in his "Ranch Life and the Hunting Trail," these wretched cow-towns were places "in which drinking and gambling are the only recognized forms of amusement, and where pleasure and vice are considered synonymous terms."

The frontier towns of the West in the cowboy period also were products of the conditions that existed. A transformation was in progress. Civilization was pushing its way onward with the irresistable force of the prodigious glaciers that in distant past ages moved over parts of the same country, and, as with these glaciers, its front was shoving ahead a morainic mass—a conglomeration of human *débris* and of harsh forces of both mankind and Nature.

Coming from the haunting and oppressive solitude and silence of the plains into these places of disorder and vice, many of the cowboys behaved as if they were dazed by the change of scene and surroundings. They were no longer the reserved, self-repressed men of the range, but threw off all restraint, and measured their "enjoyment" of their few days of freedom and revelry by the degree of uproar with which they proclaimed their presence. . . .

Beside such indoor dissipation as this, the cowboys, when in the cowtowns, would indulge in open-air demonstrations not well calculated to add to the sense of security in others who were abroad on the streets. After "loading up" with poisonous whisky, which was about the only kind sold on the frontier, a group of them would mount their ponies and put off at a gallop to "shoot up the town." Tearing up and down, yelling and whooping, and shooting here and there, or firing wildly into the air, they made themselves believe they were "seeing something of life." They might ride into a saloon and up to a bar to call for more liquor, and while waiting for it divert themselves by putting bullets through the mirrors, bottles, and other glass "furniture" of the outfit, and so bring on a mêlée in which one or more of their number would suffer from the revolvers or shot-guns of the exasperated keeper of the place and his partisans.

Nevertheless, it was not these follies, wild and foolish as they were, and that dissipated every dollar of a season's wages, that characterized these cowboys as a class. After several days of such debauchery and frolicking, those who had engaged in these "celebrations" and had not found a permanent abiding-place in the local "Boot Hill," turned their faces and their ponies rangeward and set out to resume the daily round of hard labor under conditions that were equally hard, if not harder, but in which faithfulness to duty and fidelity to their employers' interests were their foremost considerations. It was this willing faithfulness, under circumstances which put it to the most trying tests, that characterized the cowboy in filling the place that fell to him during the years in which civilization was forcing its way into and over the immense wild land of the West.

However, not all these men took part in the orgies and debaucheries of the cowtowns, or forgot themselves at other times or in other places. There were many, even in the "wildest and woolliest" period, who steadfastly held themselves aloof, kept their wits about them, saved their wages, and successfully became range-stockmen on their own account in later years.

Before the close of the period of the trail and of the open range the western cowboys had developed traits, manners, and practices that may be said to have made them a separate class of men. A large majority were native-born Americans, but in their ranks there were many young Englishmen, Irishmen, and Scotchmen, together with some of German origin. But the life brought all so close together that those of alien birth hardly were distinguishable from the others after a few years. Their manner of living and the routine of their occupation were the same from Texas to Montana; conditions then existing in the West also were much the same over the range country from far South to far North, and so the influences of these combined to impress upon this remarkable body of men a sort of "hall-mark," a distinctive and not unattractive class-stamp.

For some ten or fifteen years after the Civil War there was a considerable number of Mexican cowboys on the range, most of them being from the southern parts of the country. These were skilful men in every branch of the work and did it well, but the standing objection to them on the part of the employers was that they were rough, abusive, and unfeeling in their treatment of the stock, and personally untrustworthy. Between these and the others there seldom was any of the fraternal feeling, and usually the caste-prejudice placed the Mexicans under great disfavor from the start; a prejudice that was stronger among the Texans than among their brethren in the North, but with all it was sufficient soon to make the combination a disagreeable one.

Among these old-time cowboys the Texans and those of Texan antecedents were the most efficient for all-around work on the range and on the trail. Nearly all of them lived and moved as if they had been born in the saddle and had seldom been out of it since. They hesitated about doing anything outdoors on foot, and if they had to go but a few yards they would mount their horse for the journey—a habit, however, that was but little less fixed among the entire fraternity. While all cowboys had to be good horsemen, the Texan was, it would seem, as skilful and daring a rider as he could have been were he and his pony grown together. Of him Sweet and Knox, in their book, "On a Mexican Mustang Through Texas" (1883), in which only the amusing side of life in Texas at that time is set forth, say:

"The cowboy is a man attached to a gigantic pair of spurs. He inhabits the prairies of Texas, and is successfully raised as far North as the thirtieth degree of latitude. He is in season all the year round, and is generally found on the back of a small mustang pony, 'wild and savage as a colt of the Ukraine.' This fact has given rise to a widely diffused belief that the cowboy cannot walk; and he is often cited as an instance—a stupendous manifestation, in fact—of the wonderful working of Nature to adapt her creatures to the circumstances surrounding them. It is argued that once the cowboy was a human being,—a biped with the ordinary powers of locomotion,—but that during the course of ages, becoming more and more attached to his horse, and having gradually ceased to use his legs, these important adjuncts have been incapacitated for pedestrian uses, and thus the cowboy and his pony have developed into a hybrid union of man and horse,—an inferior kind of centaur.

"Some scientists, however, dispute this, as several specimens of the cowboy have been seen, from time to time, who, wandering into the busy haunts of man, have—under the influence of excitement, and while suffering from intense thirst—been seen to detach themselves from their mustangs, and disappear into business houses, where their wants were attended to by a man wearing a diamond breastpin and a white apron. Yet, though this was proved beyond a doubt by several competent witnesses, it was acknowledged that the specimens alluded to walked, or rather staggered, with uneven and wavering steps. This, however, does not disprove the development theory."

Between the cowboy's riding and that of the Eastern man who exhibits himself on horseback in city parks or "follows the hounds," no comparison can be made. It is only to be contrasted. It would seem that a better rider than this cattle-guarding man of the plains never lived, and certainly his ease, litheness, and gracefulness in the saddle, contrasted with the usual trussed-up, apprehensive, and sometimes simian-like, attitude of the park horseman, made the latter appear ridiculous. While the cowboy had an elaborate vocabulary of forceful adjectives at his command, he found himself unable fully to express the disdain with which he regarded the little pad-saddle—or "postage-stamp-saddle"—and the short-hitched stirrups of the conventional rider. He would have none but a "real saddle," and his stirrups hung just enough above the lengths of his legs to afford his feet a firm hold in them. When riding he did not perch in his stirrups, but rested his body upon the saddle and kept it there without letting daylight show under him; and, it may be remarked here, this continues to be the ranchman's mode of riding, as well as that of nearly all other Western men who have occasion to mount a horse. In his large and comfortable saddle with its long-hitched stirrups the cowboy could do with ease and grace all that is possible to the conventional horseman, beside a multitude of things that the latter would not dare to attempt.

The cowboys' garb added much to their "picturesqueness" in

177

the eyes of those who came from afar; and, indeed it was picturesque. As individual tastes among them varied only as to details,
their working costume was about the same in every part of the
cattle country, excepting in winter on the central and Northern
ranges, when and where more "bundling up" was necessary. But
everywhere, from early in the spring until late in the autumn, their
apparel was almost as much the same as the uniform of the soldiers
of the regular Army. In the period of the trails and the open-range
the cowboys in the main were young men, grizzled plainsmen only
occasionally appearing among them; and a regiment of them gathered promiscuously from Texas to Montana would have met army
requirements as to age, as well as appearing as an uniquely uni-
formed body of cavalry.

But considerations of the picturesque had nothing to do with
fixing the characteristic dress of the cowboy. This, like its wearer,
was an evolution—a product of conditions that was adapted to the
service it had to render; and its wearer had no thought of real or
imaginary theatrical effects the combination might produce. The
broad-brimmed, soft felt hat, with the brim turned up in front, was
to him the most serviceable known form of head-gear; and this and
his leather "chaps" or overalls, often of goat-skin tanned with the
hair on and worn with the hair outside, were the more conspicuous
features in the make-up of his working costume. His other clothing
was such as he found "ready-made" in the clothing stores of the
country towns. He wore a heavy, loose-fitting flannel shirt with a
handy pocket or two in it, and a large handkerchief, usually of
bright-colored silk, tied around his neck. His trousers, which were
kept in place by a belt—never by suspenders—were tucked into the
tops of his boots; but the chaps came down full length over the
trousers and boots and touched the ground—often dragging a little.
His body-covering was easy-fitting and free, but that of his feet was
quite different. Here he would wear nothing but tight-fitting boots—
the tighter the better in his estimation, and these boots must have
very high heels. Their tightness and their lofty heel had a sort of
crippling effect when he was upon the ground, and in walking he
went sometimes with a kind of toddling gait. However, as the cowboy seldom walked and never very far, his foot-gear, uncomfortable
as it would seem to have been, never troubled him much. But in the

cowboy era the wearing of high-heeled tight boots, things that are only occasionally seen nowadays, was not confined to his fraternity. They were common then, and nearly every Western man wore them, and would have considered himself quite "out of style" with any other kind on his feet—especially when he was "dressed up."

It has been said that the high heel of the cowboy's boot was for the purpose of keeping his foot from slipping forward through the stirrup, and thus putting him in an ugly predicament should he be thrown by some mishap. But as many of them had leather hoods attached to the front of their stirrups to prevent this—hoods which sometimes were very extravagant in the consumption of leather in their making—and as all cowboys refused other than high heels, this explanation seems hardly to fit the case.

However, their dress, including their favorite boots, was satisfactory to them, and, as a whole, was perfectly suited to their business in life. Their chaps were taken over from the Mexicans, but the rest of their apparel was developed by them along the lines of "natural selection."

The cowboy's strictly personal outfit was completed by the addition of a trustworthy revolver, usually of heavy caliber, that could be depended on in emergencies to open a way for daylight through the bodies of hostile creatures he encountered, including those of his own species; and a pair of huge spurs that rarely were used up to their full capacity for stirring up a horse or for punishing him. In the times when the Indians made the cowboy's daily life that of a soldier in war, as well as that of a herdsman, a carbine, or a short-barreled rifle, also was carried, slung to the saddle with the muzzle downward; and in those times he often had use for this weapon of longer range. We should not forget that this pioneer, who, in the mistaken beliefs of many people principally is associated with scenes of rowdyism in the old cowtowns, had, through many years in his career, to be a warrior of the plains as brave as the bravest, while he was also the care-taker of other men's property.

The cowboy's saddle was unlike that of most other horsemen, and among his personal belongings his chief interest centered upon it and it was the pride of his heart. It was customary in most parts of the range country for him to provide his horse-gear at his own cost, and his willingness to spend his hard-earned money for what he regarded as a fine saddle usually ran into rank extravagance. For one that had struck deep into his fancy he would eagerly give up his pay of several months, and be happy with his acquisition until some crafty saddler brought out another that out-classed it in ornateness. The old-time cowboy's saddle was a heavy, strongly-made affair, with both cantle and pommel, or horn, very high, and with large skirts. The high cantle would seem to have been of no general utility or advantage, but the high and strong pommel was a daily necessity in his business, for it came into play in various ways. When he roped a rebellious steer and brought him up short, the cowboy's end of the rope was hitched around the saddle-horn; when one of his herd of cattle mired in a bog and had to be helped out, he threw his rope over its horns, made his end fast to the saddle-pommel, started his horse, and tugged away; and when a wagon became stuck, or when the team pulling it was unable to climb a hill without assistance, the rope fast to the saddle-horn was the means of overcoming the trouble. Most of the saddles were provided either with pockets or small saddle-bags for odds and ends of things; and a blanket or two, together with a few extra garments, were carried in a roll behind the cantle in the cavalryman's fashion. About the bridle there was nothing especially noteworthy excepting the heavy curb bit, which appeared to be a rather cruel contrivance, but which was necessary in most cases in controlling the kind of horses used on the trail and the open range.

The mustang, bronco, or cayuse, by whichever name the beast happened to be called, was not, as is "popularly" supposed, the cowboy's ideal of a horse. Our friend was a good judge of horses, and was ambitious to become the owner of a fine one. For his work he took the best he could get, but, as with many others of the concerns of his hard life, he had to be content and to get along with what was available—to make the best use of the means at hand. The typical cow-horse, or pony, was, upon the whole, well adapted to his place, being tough in constitution and inured to all the hardships of life on the open plains. In his lightness of foot and quickness of motion he was far better adapted to his rough work in managing cattle than any other type of horse could have been. But, as he fed on grass alone, he did not have, size for size, the main strength of the grain-fed farm horse. Hence the need in the old times for so many horses on the range in proportion to the number of cowboys. To each of the latter, according to the work in hand, there were from six to twelve horses, to be used in turn—a circumstance in which is reflected the remarkable vigor and endurance of the man who rode them.

These cowboys were absolutely fearless riders, and the breaking in and management of their half-wild and, at the start wholly rebellious, steeds, was a job that called for skill and courage. Within recent times exhibitions of "bronco-busting" have been made a popular form of entertainment for the public in several western towns, and the young men who have participated in them have shown great skill and daring in conquering unruly horses. But this kind of business was almost a daily affair in the life of the old-time cowboy. It was only one of the things he had to do, and he did it without thinking much about it, or ever dreaming that some day it would be made the means of commanding the applause of a multitude. There were horses in every old range outfit that were as ugly and vicious when threatened with the saddle and bridle as any that ever have been seen in a "bronco-busting contest," and some that were even more so—that became habitual fighters, and pitched and plunged and bucked every time they were put under saddle. But the cowboy of that period regarded an encounter with one of these merely as an incidental duty in a day's work.

"Bronco-busting" is an ancient performance, the pioneer in it having been the prehistoric benefactor of his race, who was first to bestride a horse and show to his friends and neighbors that the beast could be made to carry a man on his back. The most famous of historical bronco-busters was Alexander the Great, king of Macedon (356–323 B.C.), who, having conquered the entire civilized world before he was thirty, wept because there were no more nations left for him to invade and subdue. When only thirteen years of age Alexander mounted and brought to terms the fiery and plunging steed, Bucephalus ("ox-head"), so called, because he had a white spot on his nose shaped somewhat like the head of an ox. Bucephalus had thrown, or "bucked" off, groom after groom, but the boy Alexander mounted and "busted" him within a few minutes—according to the story.

In the days of the open and free range the cowboy often slept on the bare ground wrapped in his blankets, taking philosophically whatever sort of treatment the elements might see fit to bestow upon him. At other times the dug-out, or the shack, or the tent, of an outlying camp afforded him some shelter. He ate his meals sitting on the ground at the tail-end of the mess, or "chuck", wagon that followed the movements of the herd, and his utensils in this service consisted of a tin plate, a tin cup, and sometimes a knife and a fork. His fare was as plain as his mode of life, but he found compensation for its lack of variety and the crudeness of his surroundings when "at table" in an appetite that had few equals and no superiors. Although he had thousands of cattle in his keeping, milk, cream, and butter practically were unknown to his commissariat. Of the range country in the old times it was said that "there are more cows and less butter, more rivers and less water, and you can see farther and see less, than in any other country in the world."

Many of the cowboys became almost as well versed in "sign" lore as the earlier plainsmen, the traders, and trappers, had to be. All manner of tracks, trails, and marks were to them data from which to draw conclusions; some peculiar movement of an animal indicated the presence of some other animal in the neighborhood; by the course and even the "feel" of the wind they forecasted changes of weather; a broken limb of a tree, a crushed weed, the *débris* around a deserted camping-place, the flight of a buzzard or other birds, were to the experienced cowboy, as they had been to the traders and trappers, what sign-boards and advertisements are to dwellers in settled communities.

In recent times the story-writers have been turning to the cattle ranches of the West for "material," and their "romances of the range" have become very popular. But the conditions in which the characters in many of these tales are represented as living and moving are far from those which surrounded the cowboy of the free range and the old trails. The average modern ranch-house is a comfortable home; generally speaking, the cattle graze unattended in fenced pastures; and the daily round of duties of the men in charge is much nearer like the routine on a large farm than to the life and work of the cowboys of the wild and open range. No matter how much there may be of "romance" in the present-time ranch-life, there was precious little of it in the experience of the range herdsman of a quarter of a century or so ago.

Of the cowboy of that period and of his decidedly unromantic life and business, Mr. Andy Adams, author of "The Log of a Cowboy" and of other Western stories, himself one of the old brotherhood, says in a recent magazine article:

"To describe the rank and file of this once splendid army of horsemen is no easy task. The same ground has been thoroughly covered before by pen and pencil and under limelight and slow curtain. To take any other than the popular view of this swaggering type, girdled with guns and rigged in the supposed regalia of the range, is to invite censure. Does the cowboy deserve credit for being a fine horseman when his work required him to be such or abandon his calling? True, the occupation was one that demanded the strenuous and weeded out the weakling. But are there no other avenues in life to-day that require daring and courage to meet the emergency with promptness and dispatch? 'Yes, but not so romantic,' some one answers. Romantic! Ask any man who ever made a trip over the trail if he was ever caught on the plains in a rain-storm with no fuel but buffalo chips. Ask him how many days passed without being able to make a cup of coffee, and did he really enjoy saturated clothing and wet blankets, and how far from the wagon would a herd drift on such a night. Ask him if he ever worked in the North, when every morning he shook the drifting snow from his blankets, and in the eye of a blizzard rode to turn a winter-drift of cattle. If he answers in the affirmative, inquire further if he was ever lifted out of a saddle, benumbed with cold, and did he really feel that the occupation was a romantic one. If still unsatisfied, ask him from a sanitary standpoint if there was anything would beat spreading his underclothing on an ant-hill to remove the vermin."

Yet for all of this, and for much more, too, his wages were not large enough to make him purse-proud, nor did they warrant the open-handed generosity of his kind. The cowboy was not what most people now would look upon as a well-paid man. Around thirty years ago, in the times when the raucous and brawling cowtowns were mazes of snares and pitfalls for him, many of his class were working for from $20.00 to $25.00 per month and "keep," such as the latter was; though the experienced trailman was paid more for his services while on the trail. But the cowboy then required that his wages be in the form of "hard money"—a stroke of business sagacity that stood out in sharp, almost comical, contrast with the foolish recklessness that was characteristic of the brotherhood as a whole in spending the money. At that time the Mexicans in the calling were content with even less, few of these receiving more than $12.00 or $15.00 per month, "and found." These also did business with their employers on a specie basis; and with many gestures of suspicion, and even of contempt, repudiated a tender of paper money for any amount. In later years the cowboy's wages moved higher notch by notch, and before railroads and wire fences had put him out of business his pay ranged from $30.00 to $40.00 by the month in the specie-basis currency of the land, with a "keep" that averaged much better than he had known in the earlier years. By this time, while he still was a generous soul, he had become much less reckless in squandering his money.

For such money-pay as that which is represented by the figures set down in the foregoing, the cowboy lived the life of which something is suggested in our quotation from Mr. Adams. For him it had a fascination that is hard for us to understand. He braved the elements in the parts of our country where their extremes are to be seen at their worst; or, at all events, where the conditions made them seem to be at their worst. If the reader ever has been abroad upon the great, lonely, grieving plains, far away from any sign of the presence of his fellow-men, when a blizzard out of the north was sweeping in fury over the land, he will recall the sense of utter desolation by which he was seized, the feeling of helplessness that bore him down in the presence of such forces in such a situation. The howling, freezing wind drives swirling, blinding sheets of shotlike sleet and powdery snow that sting and smother and blot out all the world around and wrap the hills and valleys in a winding-sheet of ice. In the opposite season, when the sun might burn and burn in a cloudless sky, week after week, even month after month, withering and shriveling the grass, glaring the land with its shimmering, blistering heat, and wasting the water of the streams and pools into nothingness, the cowboy patiently still went on with his work and did the best that was in him—for a few dollars for a month of his time, services, and for his knowing how. He liked his work, took pride in it, and knew of nothing that would or could induce him to neglect it. When the rolling clouds of the summer tempest blackened the sky, and the lightning flamed and crashed and roared, terrifying the horde of beasts that was in his keeping and startling them into the dreaded stampede, he rode forth with no thought save that of doing his duty; though he knew that Death, in a form so cruel that we shrink from thinking of it, under the hoofs of his surging and plunging herd might be waiting for him out yonder on the prairie, or be lurking at the base of the steep bank of a sandy river-bed a mile or two farther away, over which he and many of his cattle were likely to plunge to a common fate.

Many of the employers of these men were either non-residents or dwellers in the towns or cities of the States and Territories in which their herds were located. They might visit their ranches and remain a few days once or twice a year, but at all other times their property was wholly in the keeping of their cowboys under the direction of a foreman or manager, who usually was a man who had been promoted from the ranks. The success of the enterprises and even the preservation of the large capital invested in them were, so far as the conduct of affairs on the range determined these, de-pendent on the faithfulness and prompt attention to duty under all circumstances of the foreman and his cowboys. In the history of the cattle range the instances of failure to meet these exacting require-ments are few and far between.

Among these men there were many of good address and some of excellent education—young fellows who had struck out into the West to take their chances with Fortune. Whatever they may have been or done when "in town," they were as a class frank, honorable, and hospitable when on the range, although they were disposed to be quiet and reserved in their manner in the presence of strangers. But, as a rule, their silent ways were not those of moroseness. In most of them there was a grave, unostentatious courtesy toward a visitor; this being particularly noticeable in those of the South, to visitors who had come from that part of the country. Their reserve, however, fell away in their associations with each other, and, when a number of them were gathered around a camp-fire, or at ranch headquarters, or at a round-up, they were lively enough among themselves, and in their stories, sallies, and railleries there was much coarseness of language. But no more than one would hear among an equal number of miners in a western mining town; perhaps not so much, and certainly it would not be heard so often. They were strongly disposed to be clannish, and, while there were occasional feuds between individuals that usually ended in the death of one or the other, sometimes of both, as a body of men they would fight for each other to the last.

The cowboy was not a garrulous person. He had developed to a remarkable degree the faculty of expressing himself in the terse, crisp, clear-cut language of the range, and when he spoke his hearers had no good reason for misunderstanding his meaning. The long-winded and pompous speeches that have been attributed to men of his calling in some of the late-time "stories of the range" would have turned gray the hair of an old-timer had he been forced into an attempt to "get them off." Under reasonable provocation he was a profane man. Few, even among his most ardent partisans, would undertake to controvert this assertion. But he did not depend upon the commonplace, shop-worn terms of the town plodder. However, it is to be said that it was an uncommon thing for him to break forth with his full powers without fair justification. For this purpose he had a most astonishing vocabulary, and in dealing with a detestable range-horse, or in striving to make a half-wild, long-horned, obstinate steer behave himself and go the way that he should, nothing but its vigorous employment appeared to fit the circumstances of the case. For use upon such occasions, and also upon sundry others, every well-equipped cowboy of the old times had acquired and kept at his command what appeared to be the entire resources of Anglo-Saxon speech that could be worked into phases of denunciation—and they are not few in number; and when he intermingled with these an assortment of picturesque and glowing Spanish expletives and terms of approbrium, as he frequently did, the earth trembled.

But he also had vocal resources other and quite different from those of profanity for use in his rough business. Often at night when his cattle became restive under the mutterings of a coming storm, or uneasy from some unseen cause, or from the darkness of an over-clouded sky, and even when on stampede, he would sing to them. The sound of the human voice in melody, however rude this might have been, usually had, under such circumstances, a soothing, assuring, and quieting effect upon the half-wild, apprehensive beasts. It is not worth while to discuss here the whys and wherefores of it, but it had such an effect. The cowboy made no pretensions to an elaborate *repertoire*. When an occasion arose for doing so, he sang, or tried to sing, such songs as he happened to know as well as he could. Usually he knew some "church-tunes"—lingering reminiscences of his boyhood away off somewhere toward sunrise, for as a cowboy he seldom even saw a church from afar, to say nothing of going inside of one. Sometimes he recalled the words or a part of them that went with these tunes, and used them to the best advantage. The music of "Old Hundred," and the music and words of "I Would Not Live Alway" were favorites on the range in times of threatened trouble. But oftener the cowboy improvised words for these and other church-tunes, or adapted to them those of some doggerel song he knew—it was all the same to him; the cattle were affected by the music, not by the words, and to give them the music was what he was trying to do. But occasionally among these men an exquisite voice was heard, and when one of these was raised the restless cattle listened to the most real of music. Still, the typical old-time cowboy hardly could be called a singing man—there was too much strenuousness in his life for that, and so it was not very often that vocal music, or any other kind, for that matter, was heard in a cowcamp or at ranch headquarters.

It happened sometimes that the curiosity of range-stock became aroused by the singing of men at night, and the animals would draw and look on as well as listen. The French missionary, the Abbé Domenech, from whose book we have quoted in a former part of this volume, tells as follows of an early incident of this kind that occurred in 1849 while he was on one of his journeys over the valley of the Colorado River of Texas:

"It was our last night for sleeping on the plain, and this idea heightened our good humor. Pipes were lighted, conversation became animated, we wrapped our cloaks about us, looked up to the heavens, and sang in concert such as memory recalled of the hymns and melodies which had been familiar to us in our childhood. At two o'clock in the morning we ceased singing, * * * ; but what was our surprise on finding that we were surrounded by Americans, Irishmen, and Mexicans, who had drawn near to hear us sing; behind them we saw a regular troop of horses and oxen [cattle], forming a circle around us, having also no doubt been attracted by our singing."

As we have remarked heretofore, railroads and wire fences brought to an end the business, the rough life, and the stormy career of the old-time cowboy. Before 1890 the great cattle-trails had ceased to be cattle-trails, and grass was reclaiming their ways. The former tumultuous cowtowns had become mere way-station shipping-points with competitors every few miles along the railroads, and some of them had entered upon the decline that afterward reduced them to the dimensions of hamlets. Everywhere the range was being divided up into pasture-lots, enclosed by wire fences, in which gentler kinds of cattle, new to the country, quietly were grazing. For the old-time cowboy of the trail and the open-range the beginning of the end was at hand.

His successors in the cattle business in the West keep up some of the customs and traditions of the old life. With most of them the dress is much the same, barring the rather frequent appearance of the white shirt. They ride cow-ponies—and do it well—and use about the same kind of saddle, though the rope and saddle-pommel are not put to so many uses now. Sometimes an outlying village in the ranch country is stirred up a little by a bunch of them, but these affairs are mild echoes of what used to be done, and, like the old practice of carrying a big revolver all the time and everywhere, this has fallen into much disfavor. In some parts of Wyoming and of Montana, and more in Arizona, the departure from the old ways has not moved quite so far, and there only are lingering semblances to these yet to be seen. But broadly speaking, life on the western cattle-ranches now is, as we have mentioned in passing, much nearer like that on a great well-managed farm than that of the old days when the range was open and "free."

Mr. Hough concludes his exquisitely told "Story of the Cowboy" —the old-time cowboy, a story written in 1896, that every reader of these pages may peruse with pleasure and profit, with the following:

"Singularly enough, at the time of the writing of these lines, there is in progress in a city in western Nebraska a great 'irrigation fair,' the first of its kind in the history of that part of the country. This fair exploits the possibilities of the soil when under irrigation. Thousands of people have come together there, among these many

Indians and cowboys and old-time men of the plains. In faint imitation of the days of the past, the town is run 'wide open.' It is reported that the scenes of '69 and '70 are repeated. The cowboys are riding their horses into the saloons as they did in the days of the early drives. It is sought to revive the spirit of that old West, which is really dead beyond the reach of all our lamentations. Do many pause to consider how dramatic a scene this really is, this irrigation fair, at which the cowboy is asked to attend as a curiosity, as an attraction? Does he himself know what it is that they are asking him to do? They ask him to disport himself in a Titanic shadow-dance, and to close his play by blowing into its final flare the dwindling flame of his own candle.

"The West has changed. The old days are gone. The house-dog sits on the hill where yesterday the coyote sang. The fences are short and small, and within them grow green things instead of gray. There are many smokes now rising over prairie, and they are wide and black instead of thin and blue.

"As we look out in the evening light from where we stand, we may see the long shining parallels of the iron trail reaching out into the sunset. A little busy town lies near, flanked with fields of grain ready for the harvesting. There are cattle; but not those of 'deformed aspect' which Coronado saw when he walked across this country in the gray of other days, but sleek, round beasts, which stand deep in crops their ancestors never saw. In the little town is the hurry and bustle of modern life, even here, upon the extreme edge of the well-settled lands. For this is in the West, or what is now known as the West. It is far out upon what may now, as well as any place, be called the frontier, though really the frontier is gone. Guarding its ghost, watching over its grave, here stands a little army post, once one of the pillars, now one of the monuments of the West.

"The routine of the uncomplaining men who make the army goes on here still, as it does all over the land. One has seen the forming of troops to-day, the over there upon the parade ground. As evening comes he can hear the song of the trumpets, music to tingle in his hair. As the sun drops to the edge of the plains there comes the boom of a cannon at the fort, and fluttering down its staff falls the flag which waves over East and West and South and North alike, alike over the present and the past.

"Out from the little 'settlement' in the dusk of the evening, always being toward where the sun is sinking, rides a figure we should know. He threads the little lane among the fences, following the guidance of hands other than his own, a thing he would once have scorned to do. He rides as lightly and as easily as ever, sitting erect and jaunty in the saddle, his reins held high and loose in the hand whose fingers turn up daintily, his whole body free yet firm in the saddle with the seat of the perfect horseman. His hat still sweeps up and back in careless freedom of fashion. It is dusk, and we may not see his trappings. Let us hope his belt is still about his waist, his spurs still jingling as he rides. His pony is the same or much the same as when we saw it many years ago coming up the street of a very different town. It trots steadily forward, with the easy movement of the animal accustomed to long distances. The two, man and horse, show up strongly in the unreal light of evening on the plains. They seem to rise and move strangely as one looks, seem to grow strangely large and indistinct. Yet they melt and soften and so define; and at length, as the red sun sinks quite to the level of the earth, the figures of both show plainly and with no touch of harshness upon the western sky.

"The cowboy as he rides on, jaunty, erect, virile, strong, with his eye fixed perhaps on the ridge miles away, from which presently there may shine a small red light to hold his gaze, now looks about him at the buildings of the little town. As the boom of the cannon comes, and the flag drops fluttering down to sleep, he rises in his stirrups and waves his hat to the flag. Then toward the edge, out into the evening, he rides on. The dust of his riding mingles with the dusk of night. We cannot see which is the one or the other. We can only hear the hoof-beats passing, boldly and steadily still, but growing fainter, fainter, and more faint."

Andy Adams

"Dead tough men bawled like babies"

1906

Andy Adams knew the cowboy perhaps better than anyone else who wrote about him. In *The Log of a Cowboy,* Adams was concerned with the details of trail driving; in later books he explored particular aspects of cowboy life in greater depth. The cowboy penchant for storytelling was demonstrated admirably by Adams in *Cattle Brands: A Collection of Western Camp-Fire Stories.* This selection is taken from the story "Around the Spade Wagon." The story is plotless and episodic, consisting of a series of interpolated narratives which suggest something of the humor and poignancy of cowboy life.

These old cronies from boyhood sparred along in give-and-take repartee for some time, finally drifting back to boyhood days, while the harshness that pervaded their conversation before became mild and genial.

"Have you ever been back in old San Saba since we left?" inquired Edwards after a long meditative silence.

"Oh, yes, I spent a winter back there two years ago, though it was hard lines to enjoy yourself. I managed to romance about for two or three months, sowing turnip seed and teaching dancing-school. The girls that you and I knew are nearly all married."

"What ever became of the O'Shea girls?" asked Edwards. "You know that I was high card once with the eldest."

From Andy Adams, "Around the Spade Wagon," in *Cattle Brands: A Collection of Western Camp-Fire Stories* (Boston, Houghton Mifflin Company, 1906), 191–200, 206–11.

"You'd better comfort yourself with the thought," answered Babe, "for you couldn't play third fiddle in her string now. You remember old Dennis O'Shea was land-poor all his life. Well, in the land and cattle boom a few years ago he was picked up and set on a pedestal. It's wonderful what money can do! The old man was just common bog Irish all his life, until a cattle syndicate bought his lands and cattle for twice what they were worth. Then he blossomed into a capitalist. He always was a trifle hide-bound. Get all you can and can all you get, took precedence and became the first law with your papa-in-law. The old man used to say that the prettiest sight he ever saw was the smoke arising from a 'Snake' branding-iron. They moved to town, and have been to Europe since they left the ranch. Jed Lynch, you know, was smitten on the youngest girl. Well, he had the nerve to call on them after their return from Europe. He says that they live in a big house, their name's on the door, and you have to ring a bell, and then a nigger meets you. It must make a man feel awkward to live around a wagon all his days, and then suddenly change to style and put on a heap of dog. Jed says the red-headed girl, the middle one, married some fellow, and they live with the old folks. He says the other girls treated him nicely, but the old lady, she has got it bad. He says that she just languishes on a sofa, cuts into the conversation now and then, and simply swells up. She don't let the old man come into the parlor at all. Jed says that when the girls were describing their trip through Europe, one of them happened to mention Rome, when the old lady interrupted: 'Rome? Rome? Let me see, I've forgotten, girls. Where is Rome?'

" 'Don't you remember when we were in Italy,' said one of the girls, trying to refresh her memory.

" 'Oh, yes, now I remember; that's where I bought you girls such nice long red stockings.'

"The girls suddenly remembered some duty about the house that required their immediate attention, and Jed says that he looked out of the window."

"So you think I've lost my number, do you?" commented Edwards, as he lay on his back and fondly patted a comfortable stomach. "Well, possibly I have, but it's some consolation to remember that that very good woman that you're slandering used to give me the glad hand and cut the pie large when I called. I may be out of the game, but I'd take a chance yet if I were present; that's what!"

They were singing over at one of the wagons across the draw, and after the song ended, Bradshaw asked, "What ever became of Raneka Bill Hunter?"

"Oh, he's drifting about," said Edwards. "Mouse here can tell you about him. They're old college chums."

"Raneka was working for the '–B Q' people last summer," said Mouse, "but was discharged for hanging a horse, or rather he discharged himself. It seems that some one took a fancy to a horse in his mount. The last man to buy into an outfit that way always gets all the bad horses for his string. As Raneka was a new man there, the result was that some excuse was given him to change, and they rung in a spoilt horse on him in changing. Being new that way, he was n't on to the horses. The first time he tried to saddle this new horse he showed up bad. The horse trotted up to him when the rope fell on his neck, reared up nicely and playfully, and threw out his forefeet, stripping the three upper buttons off Bill's vest pattern. Bill never said a word about his intentions, but tied him to the corral fence and saddled up his own private horse. There were several men around camp, but they said nothing, being a party to the deal, though they noticed Bill riding away with the spoilt horse. He took him down on the creek about a mile from camp and hung him.

"How did he do it? Why, there was a big cottonwood grew on a bluff bank of the creek. One limb hung out over the bluff, over the bed of the creek. He left the running noose on the horse's neck, climbed out on this overhanging limb, taking the rope through a fork directly over the water. He then climbed down and snubbed the free end of the rope to a small tree, and began taking in his slack. When the rope began to choke the horse, he reared and plunged, throwing himself over the bluff. That settled his ever hurting any one. He was hung higher than Haman. Bill never went back to the camp, but struck out for other quarters. There was a month's wages coming to him, but he would get that later or they might keep it. Life had charms for an old-timer like Bill, and he didn't hanker for any reputation as a broncho-buster. It generally takes a verdant to pine for such honors.

"Last winter when Bill was riding the chuck line, he ran up

against a new experience. It seems that some newcomer bought a range over on Black Bear. This new man sought to set at defiance the customs of the range. It was currently reported that he had refused to invite people to stay for dinner, and preferred that no one would ask for a night's lodging, even in winter. This was the gossip of the camps for miles around, so Bill and some juniper of a pardner thought they would make a call on him and see how it was. They made it a point to reach his camp shortly after noon. They met the owner just coming out of the dug-out as they rode up. They exchanged the compliments of the hour, when the new man turned and locked the door of the dug-out with a padlock. Bill sparred around the main question, but finally asked if it was too late to get dinner, and was very politely informed that dinner was over. This latter information was, however, qualified with a profusion of regrets. After a confession of a hard ride made that morning from a camp many miles distant, Bill asked the chance to remain over night. Again the travelers were met with serious regrets, as no one would be at camp that night, business calling the owner away; he was just starting then. The cowman led out his horse, and after mounting and expressing for the last time his sincere regrets that he could not extend to them the hospitalities of his camp, rode away.

"Bill and his pardner moseyed in an opposite direction a short distance and held a parley. Bill was so nonplussed at the reception that it took him some little time to recollect his thoughts. When it thoroughly dawned on him that the courtesies of the range had been trampled under foot by a rank newcomer and himself snubbed, he was aroused to action.

" 'Let's go back,' said Bill to his pardner, 'and at least leave our card. He might not like it if we didn't.'

"They went back and dismounted about ten steps from the door. They shot every cartridge they both had, over a hundred between them, through the door, fastened a card with their correct names on it, and rode away. One of the boys that was working there, but was absent at the time, says there was a number of canned tomato and corn crates ranked up at the rear of the dug-out, in range with the door. This lad says that it looked as if they had a special grievance against those canned goods, for they were riddled with lead. That fellow lost enough by that act to have fed all the chuck-line men that would bother him in a year.

"Raneka made it a rule," continued Mouse, "to go down and visit the Cheyennes every winter, sometimes staying a month. He could make a good stagger at speaking their tongue, so that together with his knowledge of the Spanish and the sign language he could converse with them readily. He was perfectly at home with them, and they all liked him. When he used to let his hair grow long, he looked like an Indian. Once, when he was wrangling horses for us during the beef-shipping season, we passed him off for an Indian on some dining-room girls. George Wall was working with us that year, and had gone in ahead to see about the cars and find out when we could pen and the like. We had to drive to the State line, then, to ship. George took dinner at the best hotel in the town, and asked one of the dining-room girls if he might bring in an Indian to supper the next evening. They didn't know, so they referred him to the land-lord. George explained to that auger, who, not wishing to offend us, consented. There were about ten girls in the dining-room, and they were on the lookout for the Indian. The next night we penned a little before dark. Not a man would eat at the wagon; every one rode for the hotel. We fixed Bill up in fine shape, put feathers in his hair, streaked his face with red and yellow, and had him all togged out in buckskin, even to moccasins. As we entered the dining-room, George led him by the hand, assuring all the girls that he was per-fectly harmless. One long table accommodated us all. George, who sat at the head with our Indian on his right, begged the girls not to act as though they were afraid; he might notice it. Wall fed him pickles and lump sugar until the supper was brought on. Then he pushed back his chair about four feet, and stared at the girls like an idiot. When George ordered him to eat, he stood up at the table. When he wouldn't let him stand, he took the plate on his knee, and ate one side dish at a time. Finally, when he had eaten everything that suited his taste, he stood up and signed with his hands to the group of girls, muttering, 'Wo-haw, wo-haw.'

" 'He wants some more beef,' said Wall. 'Bring him some more beef.' After a while he stood up and signed again, George interpret-ing his wants to the dining-room girls: 'Bring him some coffee. He's awful fond of coffee.'

"That supper lasted an hour, and he ate enough to kill a horse. As we left the dining-room, he tried to carry away a sugar-bowl, but Wall took it away from him. As we passed out George turned back and apologized to the girls, saying, 'He's a good Injun. I promised him he might eat with us. He'll talk about this for months now. When he goes back to his tribe he'll tell his squaws all about you girls feeding him.'"...

Bradshaw made several attempts to go, but each time some thought would enter his mind and he would return with questions about former acquaintances. Finally he inquired, "What ever became of that little fellow who was sick about your camp?"

Edwards meditated until Mouse said, "He's thinking about little St. John, the fiddler."

"Oh, yes, Patsy St. John, the little glass-blower," said Edwards, as he sat up on a roll of bedding. "He's dead long ago. Died at our camp. I did something for him that I've often wondered who would do the same for me—I closed his eyes when he died. You know he came to us with the mark on his brow. There was no escape; he had consumption. He wanted to live, and struggled hard to avoid going. Until three days before his death he was hopeful; always would tell us how much better he was getting, and every one could see that he was gradually going. We always gave him gentle horses to ride, and he would go with us on trips that we were afraid would be his last. There wasn't a man on the range who ever said 'No' to him. He was one of those little men you can't help but like; small physically, but with a heart as big as an ox's. He lived about three years on the range, was welcome wherever he went, and never made an enemy or lost a friend. He couldn't; it wasn't in him. I don't remember now how he came to the range, but think he was advised by doctors to lead an outdoor life for a change.

"He was born in the South, and was a glass-blower by occupation. He would have died sooner, but for his pluck and confidence that he would get well. He changed his mind one morning, lost hope that he would ever get well, and died in three days. It was in the spring. We were going out one morning to put in a flood-gate on the river, which had washed away in a freshet. He was ready to go along. He hadn't been on a horse in two weeks. No one ever pretended to notice that he was sick. He was sensitive if you offered any sympathy, so no one offered to assist, except to saddle his horse. The old horse stood like a kitten. Not a man pretended to notice, but we all saw him put his foot in the stirrup three different times and attempt to lift himself into the saddle. He simply lacked the strength. He asked one of the boys to unsaddle the horse, saying he wouldn't go with us. Some of the boys suggested that it was a long ride, and it was best he didn't go, that we would hardly get back until after dark. But we had no idea that he was so near his end. After we left, he went back to the shack and told the cook he had changed his mind,—that he was going to die. That night, when we came back, he was lying on his cot. We all tried to jolly him, but each got the same answer from him, 'I'm going to die.' The outfit to a man was broke up about it, but all kept up a good front. We tried to make him believe it was only one of his bad days, but he knew otherwise. He asked Joe Box and Ham Rhodes, the two biggest men in the outfit, six-footers and an inch each, to sit one on each side of his cot until he went to sleep. He knew better than any of us how near he was to crossing. But it seemed he felt safe between these two giants. We kept up a running conversation in jest with one another, though it was empty mockery. But he never pretended to notice. It was plain to us all that the fear was on him. We kept near the shack the next day, some of the boys always with him. The third evening he seemed to rally, talked with us all, and asked if some of the boys would not play the fiddle. He was a good player himself. Several of the boys played old favorites of his, interspersed with stories and songs, until the evening was passing pleasantly. We were recovering from our despondency with this noticeable recovery on his part, when he whispered to his two big nurses to prop him up. They did so with pillows and parkers, and he actually smiled on us all. He whispered to Joe, who in turn asked the lad sitting on the foot of the cot to play 'Farewell, my Sunny Southern Home.' Strange we had forgotten that old air,—for it was a general favorite with us,—and stranger now that he should ask for it. As that old familiar air was wafted out from the instrument, he raised his eyes, and seemed to wander in his mind as if trying to follow the refrain. Then something came over him, for he sat up rigid, pointing out his hand at the empty space, and muttered, 'There stands—mother—now—under—

the—oleanders. Who is—that with—her? Yes, I had—a sister. Open—the—windows. It—is—getting—dark—dark—dark.'

"Large hands laid him down tenderly, but a fit of coughing came on. He struggled in a hemorrhage for a moment, and then crossed over to the waiting figures among the oleanders. Of all the broke-up outfits, we were the most. Dead tough men bawled like babies. I had a good one myself. When we came around to our senses, we all admitted it was for the best. Since he could not get well, he was better off. We took him next day about ten miles and buried him with those freighters who were killed when the Pawnees raided this country. Some man will plant corn over their graves some day."

As Edwards finished his story, his voice trembled and there were tears in his eyes. A strange silence had come over those gathered about the camp-fire. Mouse, to conceal his emotion, pretended to be asleep, while Bradshaw made an effort to clear his throat of something that would neither go up nor down, and failing in this, turned and walked away without a word. Silently we unrolled the beds, and with saddles for pillows and the dome of heaven for a roof, we fell asleep.

Frank Collinson

"I am glad I had the experience"

1934-43

English-born Frank Collinson began working as a cowboy on a Texas ranch in 1872 at the age of seventeen. In 1934, more than sixty years later, he began writing his reminiscences for *Ranch Romances*. That raises questions about his powers of recollection, but students of the West, J. Frank Dobie among them, have generally endorsed what he wrote. This selection, from his *Life in the Saddle*, is perhaps best read as a measure of the effect of cowboying on one man, or as a study in the romanticizing of the cowboy experience.

Since I had been working more with horses than with cattle on the Noonan ranch, I looked forward to the trail trip with John T. Lytle and his cousin, Tom McDaniel, to the Red Cloud Indian Agency at Fort Robinson on the Niobrara River in northwestern Nebraska. I respected Lytle and knew him well and believed he would treat me right. This trip would give me just the opportunity I wanted to see the country, and it spelled adventure. This too would suit me fine, as I was in my nineteenth year. I would be paid sixty dollars a month because I had seven good horses and could mount myself. Unmounted pay was thirty dollars per month. This was good money and would enable me to get ahead.

Lytle contracted in the late winter of 1873 to drive 3,500 head

From Frank Collinson, *Life in the Saddle* (ed. by Mary Whatley Clarke, Norman, University of Oklahoma Press, 1963), 31–43. Reprinted by permission of the publisher.

of good, big, aged steers to the Red Cloud Agency, delivering them not later than August 1 the following year.

When I recall that first long cattle drive to the Northwest and think of the hardships we experienced, I wonder if there was really much glamour or adventure to the trip. It was 98 per cent hard work, but I am glad I had the experience, and we helped make cattle history on that drive. We beat out a trail over sections of the country that had not been traveled before, and over which thousands of cattle would later be driven to the ranges in Montana, North and South Dakota, Wyoming, and Colorado.

I started working for Lytle in December, 1873, and during January and February we rounded up 2,500 big steers, most of them being bought in small bunches from various ranchmen. Most of those steers had been branded before, as they ranged in age from four to ten years. A few of the older animals had been branded as far back as the Civil War, but the majority had been marked in the late sixties.

Lytle ranched in the southeastern corner of Medina County and had a big pasture of several thousand acres fenced in with Shanghai posts. As the steers were gathered, they were put into this pasture. We rode over parts of Medina, Frio, and Uvalde counties gathering cattle. It was a mesquite brush country, but the grass was good and water was plentiful. There were cattle all over the country, to the Río Grande on the west, and to the Gulf Coast on the east. Many ranchmen were rounding up and trail-driving cattle both to Kansas and to California.

Lytle's outfit was not considered a big one. It consisted of a dozen men, a cook, and a horse herder. When we started out rounding up we had no chuck wagon. We camped as a rule by some big stout corral, and our beds were thin. Chuck consisted of corn bread, coffee, and beef, with home-cured mast-fed bacon.

The work was rough, and it took rough men to handle those brush steers. Our work was mostly holding and driving in. We started early each morning. We would work the country and round up a bunch, then drive to the herd that was already being held. Then we'd work back to the corral, pen the ones we wanted to keep, and let the others go. Some of us usually stood guard around the corral. After a day or two, when we had a herd gathered, we would move five or ten miles to another corral. Several hundred steers would be gathered in a week's time, and we'd work back to the pasture and spend a day road-branding. We would crowd a rough pole chute full of those steers and commence to brand. A 7D, branded lengthwise on the left loin, was Lytle's road brand. After the cattle were branded they were turned into pasture, and we'd start out the next day in another direction to begin rounding up another herd.

I expected the cattle to be wilder than they really were, but they were accustomed to seeing men on horses and were fairly easily handled. Some of the aged steers were hard to hold. They would run together and make a beeline for the brush. This problem was solved by driving the holding herd to where these wild steers would be likely to run out. When they were back in the herd again, they usually cooled down. One or two real outlaws had to be roped and held until the herd was driven to them before they were turned loose again. A steer that was run and roped and jerked around was called a "windsucker." The wildest steers usually settled down upon finding themselves back with the herd after their first run.

We had several Indian scares when gathering those steers, but luckily no one was killed. Once Willie Lytle, a nephew of John T. Lytle, and I were making a trip from our camp to the Lytle ranch. Deer were thick and he shot a fat yearling doe with his Colt. After cleaning the animal, we tied it behind my saddle and rode on. A small bunch of Indians suddenly broke out of the brush and started after us, yelling at the top of their voices. "Cut that deer loose and let it go," Lytle said. This I did, and the fresh venison fell to the ground as we dashed on. When the Indians reached the meat they stopped. They must have been hungry. That was the last we saw of them.

Eighteen men, some of them veteran trail hands, left the Lytle ranch on March 16, 1874, with that herd of big steers, headed for Comanche Creek in Mason County where Lytle would receive one thousand more. We had around one hundred horses in the *remuda* and two experienced horse wranglers. We had a regular trail outfit by now, including a mess wagon, driven and bossed by the cook, and pulled by four good horses. Our bedding was also carried in this wagon, which Lytle had laid the law down about overloading. He said the roads would be rough and if the wagon was too heavy the horses could not keep up with the steers. As a consequence our bedding was rather thin—one pair of blankets, an old soogan, and a wagon sheet to each man. We slept two to a bed and doubled our supplies and were comfortable enough, unless it rained and our beds got soaked, which was often the case.

"Lick" (sorghum molasses) was the only dessert we had in the chuck wagon, and that with cured bacon, frijoles, bread, and coffee constituted our regular chuck. But we supplemented our meat diet with fresh antelope and buffalo all the way and fared fine.

On the very first night out we had the worst stampede of the entire trip. The cattle had been driven across the Medina River below Castroville and were bedded down in open prairie. They were nervous and high-strung and continued to jump up and mill around. We never knew what scared them, but before we realized what had happened they were up and dashing wildly into the night. It was hopeless to round them up before morning. The next day we gathered them all together again, with the exception of about fifty head, and felt lucky. Then we headed out for Comanche Creek in Mason County, where we would receive and brand the one thousand head to be delivered there.

On our way to Mason County we passed old Camp Verde on the edge of Kerr County, which was an interesting place to me. About twenty years before, in the late fifties before the Civil War, the United States government had imported a herd of camels from Arabia, believing they would make fine pack animals in the arid Southwest. But their feet could not stand the rocks and they were a failure. The camels were kept at this old fort before they were sent to Fort Davis and into Arizona. They were eventually turned loose to roam at will over the country. Some were caught and sold to circuses; others were taken into Mexico.

After reaching Comanche Creek in Mason County, it took us three days to receive and brand the 1,000 head received there. After this work was done three of the cowboys left us, leaving twelve men to handle the cattle, which was sufficient. At last we were headed for Fort Robinson in Nebraska, with over 3,600 steers. Each day found the herd more accustomed to the trail and less restless since the home range was behind.

We reached Fort Griffin in Shackelford County the last of April and rested up a few days on Collins Creek. We bought fresh supplies in that thriving frontier town, alive with soldiers, teamsters, and the first of the buffalo hunters.

Since we planned to head across unknown country from Griffin to Camp Supply, Indian Territory, with the first herd of cattle to be pointed in that direction, the government furnished us a guide, Champ Means, who well knew the country, the watering places, etc. He had been with General Mackenzie for two years. This was a great help to us and enabled us to reach Camp Supply without too much delay.

Our greatest trouble with the herd was stampedes, and it always took several days for them to settle down afterward. They seemed to stampede more on the drive from Fort Griffin to Camp Supply than anywhere along the trail. Maybe it was the atmosphere. Sometimes on a clear night the cattle would be bedded down, when the air would suddenly become warm and still. Then distant thunder could be heard and phosphorous would shine on the long horns of the cattle and on the horses' ears. Then we knew a storm was brewing. Suddenly like a streak of lightning every steer jumped to its feet and was away on the run. The entire herd seemed to move like one huge animal.

In such instances the cowboys tried to keep in the lead so that the steers could eventually be turned in a circle. If the lightning and thunder and rain continued, the frightened animals would keep running for several miles.

Finally when they were herded there was water standing everywhere, and it was difficult or impossible to bed them again. Then the cowboys, cold and miserable, and often wet to the skin, stood guard the remainder of the night. Maybe one or two broke into song, but it took a brave lad to sing under such conditions.

The big job awaited us at the crack of dawn. We first counted the cattle, and if any were gone, we followed their tracks on fresh horses. Maybe they were not far off—maybe they were twenty miles; but get them we had to do, even if they were half-way back to the home range.

It was my job to ride ahead of the herd from Griffin to Camp Supply to watch out for buffalo herds and keep them off our trail.

Lytle was afraid the running buffalo would stampede our cattle, and stressed the importance of finding a good bed ground where the steers would be comparatively safe from such an attack. I learned on that trip that buffalo, like cattle, would lie down at night to rest. On some days I saw big herds; and other days just a few stragglers. This was the first time that I, and several of the other cowboys, had ever seen buffalo, and we were all greatly interested in them.

One of the boys, a strapping Castroville youth, swore he was going to rope a big buffalo bull. The old hands urged him not to risk it, but he stuck to his plan, despite the fact that he rode a small horse that did not weigh over eight hundred pounds. His opportunity came a few days later when a bunch of big buffalo bulls ran through the herd and one of the animals ran by this chap. He sent his lasso flying and caught the big shaggy around the neck, but the powerful bull rushed on, jerking the horse and rider, like toys, to the ground. Luckily the Castroville cowpuncher was uninjured and quickly cut the rope with his knife. That was the last I heard on the trip about roping a buffalo bull.

Later I saw many young buffalo roped, but never an old bull. I saw Mexican hunters rope the two- and three-year-old bulls which they worked like ox teams in Mexico. Once they put the yoke on a buffalo, it was never taken off again until the animal was gentle or dead. After we crossed into Kansas we saw very few buffalo, and we saw none at all after crossing the Arkansas River.

We followed a plainly marked trail from Camp Supply to Fort Dodge. Grass and water were fine in the Arkansas Valley near Dodge, and it was there, too, that several of the boys saw their first train. Lytle rode ahead to examine the river and found it fordable. We planned to cross over the next day. This would be the first time the herd would have to swim.

We held the cattle out until midday, then struck for the river about a mile above Dodge City with the horses in the lead. The cattle were thirsty and anxious to get into the stream, but when they plunged in they became frightened and tried to turn back. It was too late then, and the cowboys in front, half of them on the point, got them started across. A floating log in midstream struck the lead cattle and again they tried to turn back, but the oncoming herd pushed them forward, and the animals all got across in good shape.

After the herd was safely over a few cowboys were left to hold the cattle, and the rest of us went back to help bring the chuck wagon over. We took the *remuda* back with us. Six horses were hitched to the wagon. Two of the boys fastened their saddle ropes to the lead horses' collars, while other cowboys who could swim got on the upper side of the wagon and kept it from turning over. The bed was well tied to the running gear and went over the river fine. The entire crossing was made in two hours.

We stayed two days in Dodge City, a typical Western "rag-town" in that June, 1874, when I first saw it. It was the end of the trail for many of the big cattle drives from Texas. Before that it had been headquarters for the buffalo hunters. After resting up there and buying supplies, we headed for the Platte River.

The cattle were in excellent condition. They had gained weight along the trail and often grazed as many as fifteen miles a day. On some days we traveled over twenty miles to the next watering place, and the long drive did not hurt the steers at all. Their hoofs were hard, and the rough terrain we had traveled did not bother any of them. Instead it had hardened and conditioned them. Their legs were long and strong, and they were now real veterans of the trail. Lytle was glad they could be delivered to the agency in such good condition.

The South Platte was crossed near Sterling, Colorado, a small town on the Union Pacific Railroad. The journey was continued uneventfully, and we later crossed the North Platte near Camp Clark. It was a relief to follow a well-marked government trail from that point to the Indian reservation, which we reached at the end of July. We were all glad to be at the trail's end, and pitched camp on the Niobrara River. Lytle soon rode over to talk to General George Custer, then in command at Fort Robinson, about receiving the cattle.

In the entire distance from Medina County, Texas—1,500 miles —we had not experienced too many difficulties. We had not seen an Indian, had enjoyed buffalo meat from Griffin to Dodge, and before that, after leaving Mason, Texas, had killed antelope whenever we wanted fresh meat. The antelope were curious animals. They often came right up to our herd and sometimes ran into it. They were easy to kill.

General Custer and the quartermaster rode out the next day to look over the herd, and they were real pleased with the stock and commented on their good condition. When the final count was made we had about two hundred more steers than the contract called for, but they were glad to buy those animals also. They paid Lytle an average of thirty-six dollars per head. At that price the government was able to feed the Indians very reasonably indeed.

August 1 was set as receiving day. When we had turned the cattle over to the agency the quartermaster offered any of the hands the same pay they had gotten on the trail to stay and help issue the cattle to the Indians. If they stayed as long as three months on the reservation, he would pay their return fare to Texas. I thought this sounded interesting and I decided to stay. So did several others. Lytle then settled with us, sold some of his horses to the quartermaster, and with the rest of his outfit, pulled out for Texas.

The steers were divided into three herds; two thousand of them were kept on the Niobrara where grazing was good, and where they could be issued to the Indians when needed. Eight hundred were held ten miles east, and eight hundred were driven to a range about two miles from the agency. I helped look after the latter herd, and we were ordered to corral them at night and herd them through the day. Our home was a camp house near the corrals, and we were to look after ourselves, do our own cooking and housekeeping. The government would furnish our supplies. We could carry guns as we had done along the trail, but never in any instance were we to trade with the Indians.

There were about ten thousand Indians on the reservation at that time, and Red Cloud, chief of the southern Sioux, was head chief over them all. He had subchiefs and these in turn had subchiefs, and each one was responsible for so many lodges.

The Sioux were the best looking of any Indians I ever saw. I often wondered where they got their strong, handsome features. I had an opportunity to see a great deal of this tribe when I was at Fort Robinson. The men were tall and well built. Many of them stood six feet or more, and weighed fully two hundred pounds.

When young the women were fine specimens of womanhood. They aged early because they worked so hard. They set up the tipis, moved camp, made clothing and moccasins, cooked, looked after the children and waited on the men. I noticed that the women never had over two or three children. I never saw any large families among them.

There were more women in camp than men. A warrior could have as many wives as he could feed. There were numerous widows because so many men had been killed in battle.

I often saw Red Cloud, the chief, who had learned that it was useless to fight against the white man. He was a fine-looking warrior but not as large as some of the men in his tribe. Some folks said he was a better leader than Sitting Bull. He was said to have led the fight at the Fort Phil Kearny Massacre when Captain W. J. Fetterman's entire force of men was destroyed on December 21, 1866.

During my stay on the reservation many of Red Cloud's young braves slipped off to join Sitting Bull. I am sure there were many of these southern Sioux in the Little Big Horn fight.

Once a week all of the Indians were issued beef on the hoof. We worked six days a week, and from our herd we issued about 125 head weekly. At the end of October the steers had diminished until there were not over 500 head left.

At first I was eager to see the Indians get their beef, but it became routine after a few days. It was always the same brutal, savage kill. The bucks dashed up on their horses, which they had painted in bizarre patterns. Behind them were the women with their knives, ready to skin and cut up the cattle.

Each morning the quartermaster told us how many cattle to issue. Those steers were driven into a separate pen, and we made it a point to get rid of the wild stuff first. After counting the cattle, the big gates were thrown open and out ran those wild, long-legged, long-horned steers with savage bucks at their heels, screaming and yelling. It was a tossup which was the wildest. The bucks shot arrows into the steers, cut their hamstrings with long, sharp knives, lanced them, and often jumped from their horses to fight with a particularly rambunctious animal. In all this melee I never saw an Indian get hurt. This sport was second nature to him. It was his way to kill—had been for ages past.

Finally, when the steers were all down, the Indians gorged themselves on the entrails until they could eat no more. Then the women had a feast and later skinned the animals and chopped up the meat. The hides, though badly damaged, were used for moccasin soles and ropes.

Naturally the red man's method of killing was not backed by the humane society, which raised a howl. But who could say which was the less humane—the white man's style of killing, or that of the Indian?

Some folks pity the bull in the ring at Spanish and Mexican bullfights. I pitied the old Texas longhorns that came to such a sad end, after weathering the trail so nobly. In my mind they were the real sports. They were among the wildest known cattle and made good beef. They also made good work animals and helped to haul heavy loads across the Plains. They could get along without water longer than any other cattle. They had harder and better hoofs. I'm sorry that they are gone from the range.

When the steers had all been issued, the quartermaster paid me off, and I sold my horses at $75 a head, with the exception of Walker, my first and favorite cow pony. He had served me well, both in Texas and up the trail. I hated to part with him. He was still a fine horse, but when I was offered $120 in gold for him I let him go.

I then headed for Texas by stage. Buffalo-hunting was beginning to be a popular business there, and I too had a yen to hunt the big shaggies.

The paper on which this book is printed bears the watermark of the University of Oklahoma Press and has an effective life of at least three hundred years.